Mutual Respect

Personal Responsibility

Accountability

Improved Relations

THE
STOP

IMPROVING POLICE & COMMUNITY RELATIONS

DWAYNE BRYANT

For information contact:
27 W. Wacker Dr.
Chicago, IL 60606
www.AboutTheStop.com

ISBN: 978-1530777754

Cover and interior design by Tim Fullerton, ForYouDesign

Support **T**eaching **O**f **P**rinciples

Dedication

My students and all young people:

Thank you for all of our wonderful conversations about life and strategies to reach success. I often tell people how my students keep me in tune and "hip". You have also provided great perspective and broadened my view about many things. During our time together, we have had several conversations ranging from time management and goal setting to bullying and building healthy relationships. We have also talked about the police: what to do and what not to do when you have an encounter. This book is an extension of those conversations written with you in mind. As you read this book, I want you to understand that my intention, as always, is to help you create a better future for yourself. Due to recent events, it is more crucial than ever that you read this book and take this conversation to heart.

To the wonderful parents of our youth:

I have heard many of you express concern about incidents between law enforcement and community, particularly with our youth. I wrote this book to assist you in having effective dialogue with your child. My desire is for you to be proactive in your conversations regarding your expectations for your child's future and their interactions with law enforcement.

To the hardworking men and women in blue:

For those of you who wear your badge with pride, exemplifying true professionalism and a commitment to your oath to protect and serve, this book is also dedicated to you. You are on the front lines every day. I know, firsthand, that your struggle and sacrifices are real. I applaud your efforts to keep our communities safe.

To the beat of my heart, my beloved mother:

Thank you for ALL of your sacrifices, instructions and love. Thank you for being tough and never giving up on me! I thank you for all of your prayers. You are a strong mother. Though James (dad) left you with six children, you served the difficult role of a mother, father and mentor. Because of the many lessons you taught us, I hear your voice speaking through me as I speak to my students. I am thankful that God chose you to be my first teacher on this planet called Earth.

Contents

Foreword

By Lee P. Brown, PhD

Director of the White House Office of National Drug Control Policy
President of the International Association of Chiefs of Police
Atlanta Public Safety Commissioner
Police Chief and Mayor of Houston, Texas
New York City Police Commissioner
Founding member of the
National Organization of Black Law Enforcement Executives

The nation is adversely affected by the increasingly tense relationship between police and community. The growing climate of distrust is among the biggest national challenges demanding an urgent need to act. When young people do not see the police as public servants and protectors of their community, chaos is lurking. When police officers do not view the community as a viable partner in their efforts to serve and protect, the very fabric of our society is at stake. The STOP is a book that is both timely and important. In this book, Dwayne Bryant creates a brilliant platform for constructive dialogue for both police and community. He outlines the importance of developing strategies focused on mutual respect, responsibility and accountability for improving police and community relations. Through real life police encounters, he urges the reader to take the first step towards improving any relationship: Self-awareness and sincere dialogue.

As a former Director of the White House Office of National Drug Control Policy, New York City Police Commissioner, Police Chief and Mayor of Houston, Public Safety Commissioner of Atlanta, President of the International Association of Chiefs of Police and a founder of the National Organization of Black Law Enforcement Executives, I am strongly positioned to expound on the techniques needed to aid in the improvement of this strained relationship. During my extensive career I have strived to support the delicate functional balance between effective police and community relations and how the factors addressed in this book impact such relationships.

My career in law enforcement has cemented my confidence in the belief that community policing should be the philosophy embraced by all police departments and become the manner by which order is maintained by encouraging mutual respect as essential to effective policing. Police who are viewed as a part of the community tend to have a stronger relationship with the community because they become heavily invested in such a relationship. The nation is becoming more aware that the current approach to policing is not working. Dwayne Bryant's The STOP – will ignite conversations based on the implementation of scenarios that readers can identify with and thereby facilitate the creation of a gateway to the development of sustainable solutions for improving police and community relations.

Capitalizing on his expertise as a mentor and educator, Dwayne Bryant pens "The STOP" in the most basic form while sharing information relevant to creating a road map to foster this most important dialogue. He provides information about fundamentals and what role a healthy relationship plays in maintaining respect and safety in the community. My interaction with this dynamic author left me inspired by his perpetual positive language about the shared responsibility of the police and community to promote a healthy relationship.

What is uniquely valuable about The Stop – which combines an in-depth understanding of encounters between police and community - is the sharing of perspectives of both police and community while giving food for thought as to the consequences of action, reaction and ultimately responsible choices.

Bryant allows readers to take charge of their lives as critical thinkers who can help determine the outcome of a police encounter. He also shares many anecdotes for students and adults designed to create a positive quality life.

Whether you are a parent, teacher, community leader or law enforcement officer; this book should be added to your "must read" list. I believe that the strategies outlined in the book will encourage honest dialogue and provide for the teaching of principles that will positively change lives. I am honored to have this opportunity to write a foreword to Dwayne Bryant's The STOP. His dedication to improving police and community relations shines through brilliantly.

Foreword

By David R. Bursten, Captain
Chief Public Information Officer
Indiana State Police

Life is a journey and like all journeys sometimes there are unexpected turns, detours and side trips. It makes arriving at the destination that much more interesting. My law enforcement journey started as a Military Police Officer in the U.S. Army and later as an Indiana State Police Officer, with a detour to the Santa Monica, CA, Police Department and back again with the Indiana State Police. Ultimately spending more than 20 of my 37 years as a police officer (and still going) dealing directly with news media explaining police activities at crime scenes, hostage situations and manmade as well as natural disasters.

A side trip -- the result of my assignment working with news media for two decades -- included meeting the author of this book, Dwayne Bryant. If not for Dwayne driving 85 mph in a 65 (he'll tell you how that happened), he wouldn't have been stopped by Trp. Aron Weller, thus setting into motion a sequence of events that touched more than a million people in a matter of a few short weeks. And now, with this book, Dwayne has the opportunity to touch countless more lives with his message of common sense for youth, parents, police officers and community leaders.

With this book Dwayne speaks from the heart about the importance of respect for one's self, for the rule of law and how a person's actions can impact – for better or worse – encounters with law enforcement. He sets the tone that both the person being stopped and the police officer making the stop have a responsibility to be respectful. His message is one you expect would be taught at home by loving and caring parents; but too often, it isn't.

The beauty and simplicity of this book is you can "hear" Dwayne speaking to you through his book. He provides a road map for a parent, teacher, or caring adult to have the important conversation about what to do and how to act if stopped by a police officer.

The Stop is written for ALL Americans. It transcends race and religion with the common sense message of respect that is reinforced over and over with real life examples that are instructive to all walks of life.

Dwayne pulls no punches speaking to the fact that police have as much responsibility, if not more, to ensure a traffic stop doesn't unduly escalate into something negative. At the same time he clearly explains the actions some citizens take that unnecessarily escalates a traffic stop to an arrest, or worse.

If you read this book and take the message to heart, you'll find that besides transcending race, the message of this book is instructive in dealing with and getting along with people; and you don't even have to have been driving a car! But if you are driving a car and you meet a police officer as the result of an action you took while driving, then take Dwayne's guidance to heart and put it to work. If you do, will it guarantee you get a warning? Not necessarily. But it will certainly enhance that possibility or maybe result in being cited for a lesser violation. After all, it all comes down to the Golden Rule of treating others the way you'd want to be treated in a similar situation.

Preface

The current climate of police and community relations is very tense. Seemingly every week, the media captures another story of a police officer's use of excessive or unreasonable force. Police officers have also been the target of random attacks and shootings, which has further reinforced the level of distrust between the police and communities.

Whether it is police against community or community against police, this chaotic relationship will prove detrimental to our communities if we continue in this manner. I sincerely believe our communities and police need each other; however, if we don't make a mutual commitment to foster honest and open dialogue and improve our efforts to bridge the gap to create a positive relationship, I am concerned that our society is headed in an irreversible direction.

It is my earnest hope that this book serves as a tool to facilitate discussion and direct action. With this purpose in mind, I would like to address the following groups:

- **Parents:** I encourage you to read this book with your children.
- **Schools:** I urge you to allow time for teachers to review this content with their students.
- **Faith-based and community organizations:** I recommend that you set aside time to discuss each chapter with your audience.
- **Law enforcement:** It is my wish that you read this book to gain insight from another perspective – one that respects law enforcement but also acknowledges that there are some troubling elements within law enforcement and community that must be addressed. From my experience, all parties must operate within the realm of respect during a police encounter.

Building mutual respect between self, community and authority should be a universal aim. Let's start with the basics: personal responsibility, integrity, collective action and accountability.

It is time we STOP and LISTEN to one another: parents to their children; teachers/administration to their students; and faith-based organizations and police to the community. I believe quality communication can help end all wars and heal all relationships. If we have the courage to sit down and talk to one another in truth, sincerity and without judgment, we can reconstruct a more Perfect Union.

According to the U.S. Bureau of Labor Statistics[1], from 2010 to 2014, parents had deliberate conversations with their children for only three minutes a day, and they read to their kids for 2.4 minutes per day. Based on these statistics, it is clear that many parents are not having proactive conversations with their children about life, nor are they sharing their expectations for when and if their children have a police encounter.

Parents share a common desire to have their children return home safely. From my experience of working directly with them, I discovered that many parents and guardians really don't know how to proactively engage their children on this topic. I want to harness the emotion and develop a sound action plan for every police encounter.

The STOP will help young people, parents, teachers and police engage in constructive dialogue about real-life issues. It encourages quality conversations to stimulate thinking and intelligent action. The STOP provides a framework for parents and teachers to engage in meaningful conversations with their children about their goals and expectations for life. It also outlines a specific strategy and action items for young people to follow during an encounter with law enforcement.

In this book, I share seven personal encounters with law enforcement. Some were awesome while others were not so great. However, I learned lessons from each of them – lessons that have proven to be effective when dealing with law enforcement, authority and life in general. I believe my experiences are valuable lessons that parents can discuss with their children. I also believe that law enforcement can utilize this book to gain insight on how to better engage the public. It is time for all parties to actively engage in reconstructing police and community relations.

The STOP provides real-life solutions to improve police and community relations. Each chapter ends with a Reflections section that offers various viewpoints from The STOP. After Reflections, several questions for young people, parents and law enforcement are provided to encourage discussion.

My question to you: Are you ready to start the dialogue?

I hope your answer is yes. If so, I challenge you to join me in starting a real and honest conversation about mutual respect, personal responsibility, integrity, collective action and accountability.

Buckle your seat belts...

About the Author

"Before You Can Change Your World, You Must Change Your Vision." - DB

Dwayne Bryant is an internationally renowned author, transformational speaker and TV personality and the founder and CEO of Inner Vision International, Inc. Known for his high energy, wit and honest storytelling ability, Bryant fuels audiences by sharing his credo of hard work, perseverance, integrity and applied faith, which are the keys to his success.

Bryant is also an award-winning author of The Vision® curricula, which teaches Social Emotional Learning and Life Management Skills to third – 12th graders. In an effort to share his messages with as many young people as possible, he serves as a keynote speaker, workshop trainer and consultant for various school districts and youth organizations.

Bryant has reached over 400,000 individuals through his motivational speaking and writings. He is sought after by corporations, nonprofits and academic institutions for his proven ability to offer step-by-step resources to audiences on how to unlock their unlimited potential.

In an effort to increase his support for improving police and community relations, Inner Vision International is donating 20% of The STOP's profits to the following charitable organizations:

- Partnering police youth charities that build community and youth awareness of law enforcement.

- Partnering Urban Leagues that focus on building youth's academics and self-esteem.

- Jan's Haven, established to empower youth within the Caribbean and Africa with a focus on sustainability using sports, music and arts.

- Inner Vision International Foundation which develops curricula, educational apps, motivational products for third graders – freshman in college.

For more information about Dwayne Bryant, please visit:
www.DwayneBryant.com
www.Inner-Vision-International.com
www.AboutTheStop.com

Introduction
The STOP Challenge

Before I approach a stop sign, I slow my vehicle down. As I get closer, I come to a complete stop. I look to my left and to my right to check for pedestrians, other vehicles or any approaching danger. If everything is clear and safe, I proceed with caution to resume driving to my destination.

This book is entitled The STOP because I want you to STOP and THINK every time you have an encounter with a police officer or any law enforcement official. You need to observe your surrounding area and proceed carefully. Imagine yourself approaching the encounter as if you were driving toward a stop sign. Start by looking to your left and right. This simply means observing two people as you come to a full stop: first yourself and then the officer.

Both you and the officer should be in the right frame of mind, being prepared to create mutual respect; thereby guaranteeing a successful stop. Ultimately, both of your objectives are to get home safely.

You may not know why you were stopped. Establish the foundation for the encounter by being polite and respectful. As you "look to your left" and "look to your right", think more about your future during the encounter and understand that your past may come into play. If your past is clean, you should have nothing to worry about. However, if there are some questionable things in your background, I want you to pay closer attention to this book.

After you have looked both ways and observed yourself and the officer, proceed with caution by allowing respect to guide your entire conversation and your actions, even if that same respect is not returned. If you feel disrespected or belittled, your feelings may be valid. Once you make it home safely, you can always devise a plan of action.

Young People:

I had an encounter with a police officer that went viral. I received thousands of emails and friend requests on Facebook. While 95% were very positive, the remaining 5% were quite negative. Some people insisted that advising young people to respect the police at all times is "crazy" and would get them killed. I do not agree with them. I believe being respectful is always the best approach even if it is not returned, especially when dealing with law enforcement.

This is why I wrote this book. I wanted to share my personal experiences, including seven encounters with law enforcement. These encounters began in elementary school and transpired throughout my adult life. Some of those encounters resulted in serious injury and could have ended in death, while others were mutually respectful and civil. In each encounter, I had to use all of the tools I am sharing with you. Often times, a successful encounter depends upon your response. From this day forward, let's ensure that your encounters will produce positive outcomes to the best of your ability.

I challenge you to read this book and share it with your friends. Make sure they also understand the importance of respect for authority (even if respect is not given in return). Please note: I am not suggesting that showing respect will always guarantee a positive outcome with your law enforcement encounter; however, I am suggesting that being respectful will guarantee you are being your best self and that will increase your probability of creating a positive encounter. At the end of the day, I want you to "make it home" and have a beautiful life.

Parents:

During a parent engagement, I was discussing how to create positive change within society. Feeling frustrated, one mother stood up and said she wished her son could drive her car without being pulled over unnecessarily and harassed by the police.

I understood her concern. Although this book does not guarantee that your sons and daughters will not get harassed or be subjected to an overuse of force, it is a helpful resource for you to talk, teach and prepare your child for encounters with law enforcement. It will allow you to have better conversations and equip your children with more tools in their success tool belt. I challenge you to speak to your children. Also, get to know their friends. Do not assume the morals and values you have instilled within your children are shared by their friends. I have witnessed good kids, from good homes be influenced negatively by their peers.

Parents, YOU are your child's first teacher. Let's teach our children how to positively engage with law enforcement. Therefore, if they have an encounter, they will be prepared. They will know how to respond with confidence and wisdom, thereby reducing fear-driven and irresponsible actions that may cause negative consequences. We do not want our children unnecessarily stopped or harassed by police. But we do want them equipped with the knowledge to make wise decisions that can result in more positive encounters.

Law Enforcement:

Some of my unpleasant encounters with law enforcement mostly occurred because the police officer unfairly profiled me or used inappropriate language, tone, and/or excessive gestures. I believe their actions were unnecessary for the situation. In retrospect, I am sure I contributed to things escalating beyond the point to which it needed. I ask you to consider the young people who will read this book in an effort to help bridge the gap between law enforcement and community.

A recent study found that many officers see Black teens as adults. However, please note that the overwhelming majority of all teens, whether Black, White, Hispanic or Asian, do not have the mental capacity of an adult. Their prefrontal cortex, which controls short-term decision making, focus, judgment and impulse control, has yet to fully develop. Regardless of their

3

physical stature, these are teens who make emotional decisions just as we once did. Teens' emotional response mechanism develops faster than judgment and logic. Simply put: teens don't always make the best decisions.

I challenge you to continue to uphold the law even when it does not seem popular to do so. Continue operating in the highest standard being a true light to our communities. I believe the majority of people are good, decent people, whether community or law enforcement.

Community:

In my opinion, most people want to believe and support law enforcement. We have to end the "us" vs. "them" mentality unless it is going to be: "us" – good and respectful citizens and law enforcement vs. "them" – bad seeds within the community and law enforcement.

If it is going to be "us" versus "them," then let all of us quality human beings join forces to expose those elements that would rather create chaos than order. Respect should be mutual in every encounter we have with law enforcement.

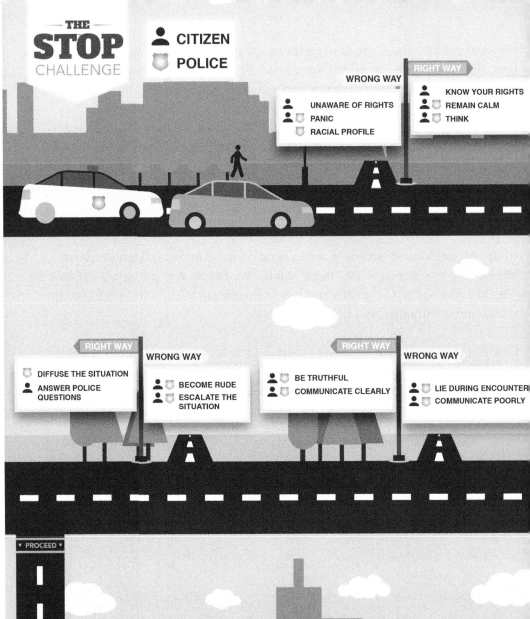

Chapter 1
My 1st Encounter: Borrowed Bikes

Dwayne's siblings singing together

Growing up in a single parent home with six siblings left us without many luxuries. My mother often times worked two to three jobs just to make ends meet. She was an avid proponent of getting a quality education and "pulling yourself up by your own boot straps." Though she qualified, she looked down upon government handouts. Her pride never allowed her to accept welfare. When I asked her about taking welfare, she said she did not want the state to tell her what she could and could not do. She disliked the idea of having her destiny controlled or being limited by external circumstances.

Due to our lack of luxuries, like a bicycle to ride freely down the street, my brother and I would rush out to the bicycle racks after the school bell rang to search for unlocked bikes. We wanted to experience the freedom that came along with riding a bicycle. Our mother was always late picking us up, so we figured we would ride around a couple of blocks and then return the bikes before someone noticed them missing.

On one particular day, the sun shone perfectly through the beautiful cumulus clouds. The wind blew gently. The temperature felt like the high 70s. As we raced down the street, we decided to go a little further. One block. Then another. We then decided to see who could go the fastest. Caught up in the pleasure of having a bike to ride, we realized we stayed out much longer than normal and had to head back immediately. As we raced to get back to the school, we noticed a police officer following us. After another block, we saw the flashing lights.

The STOP.

The police sounded his sirens. At first it was a little scary. The lights flashed and the sirens blared. We heard his voice on his megaphone saying, "You two. Pull those bikes over!" We pulled over.

Now looking back on the situation, we were on someone else's bike. We did not look at it as stealing. We had done this many times and always brought the bikes back. This time, however, we stayed out too long.

"Are those your bikes?" the police officer asked.

We quickly answered, "No sir. They belong to some of our classmates. We attend Lake Sybellia Elementary." In hindsight, we clearly had taken some-one else's property without their permission, which constitutes theft; how-ever, in our minds, we did not steal. We had just borrowed someone's bike for a few minutes, and we planned to return them to the exact same location.

The officer then told us that a bike was reported stolen, and it matched the exact description of one of the bikes we were riding. We assured the officer that we would never steal someone's bicycle. "We were only riding it until our mother came to pick us up – and she's always late," we told him.

The officer asked for our mother's telephone number. He called her at work. At that exact moment, we knew we were in trouble. Suddenly it seemed like my mother was right around the corner. She was never able to pick us up on time, but she got there fast on that day.

Once my mom arrived, the officer explained to her that the bicycles we were riding were reported stolen. She assured the officer she taught her children stealing would never be tolerated. Mom asked the officer to pardon the offense. "Please officer, don't put my sons in the back of your squad car, and please do not put your handcuffs on my boys. They are good boys." She assured him it would never happen again.

He asked her how she knew this, and she explained, "After I finish beating their A-swiggle swiggles, they won't pick up anything else that belongs to someone else ever in life."

He told my mom, "Ma'am, you can't beat your children."

My mom then said something interesting that I still remember to this day.

"Officer, I'm going to beat their A-swiggles because if I don't, you will be beating them with a Billy club or shooting them in their backs. I would rather beat them than have you kill them." As I listened to my mother speak to the police officer, I couldn't understand why he would shoot us for riding a classmate's bicycle. WOW! That was back in the early 80's, before cell phones and social media.

I did not realize it at that time, but my mother feared that something could have gone terribly wrong. Unlike today, my brother and I had no fear of losing our lives because of a police encounter.

Luckily, we had one of Maitland's finest officers because he saw my brother and myself as children. He saw my mother as a respectful parent. Maybe he had kids our age. The bottom line is he did not arrest us. He did not ruin our lives by putting us in juvenile detention. We got a warning, and to this day, I have never taken something that belonged to someone else.

Reflections

Siblings: Jackie, Michael and Dwayne

Taking something that belongs to someone else does constitute theft. Our reason for "borrowing" the item really doesn't matter. If it doesn't belong to us, it is not ours to take, "borrow" or use without the expressed permission of the owner, whether it is a pencil, a piece of paper or a bicycle.

This is a crucial conversation you must discuss with your children. We can no longer assume they always know right from wrong. Adult common sense is not always so common to children.

As I reflect back on the "borrowed bikes," many things could have gone wrong that day. My brother and I could have been rude and disrespectful to the officer. We could have jumped off the bicycles and ran instead of stopping. The officer could have used bad judgment and arrested us. Even worse, he could have shot us in our backs while we were running away in fear. My mother could have been rude and disrespectful to the officer, causing him to change his mind about arresting us. Do you see how every individual involved in the encounter has a responsibility to ensure it goes well? The police officer alone is not the only person with responsibility during The STOP.

Thankfully, the officer who stopped my brother and I viewed us as we were: young, innocent children who were unaware of the full impact of our actions. We were just having fun until our mother came to pick us up, not intending to cause any harm to anyone or anything. On the other hand, had the officer viewed us as adults, he may have used excessive and lethal force, which aligned with my mother's justified fears of her boys experiencing police brutality.

According to a recent study conducted by Harvard educated Phillip Atiba Goff, PhD[2], Black boys as young as 10 may not be viewed in the same light of childhood innocence as their White peers. Instead, they are more likely to be mistaken as older, perceived as guilty and face police violence if accused of a crime, according to new research published by the American Psychological Association.

According to Dr. Goff, "Children in most societies are considered to be in a distinct group with characteristics such as innocence and the need for protection. His research found that Black boys can be seen as responsible for their actions at an age when White boys still benefit from the assumption that children are essentially innocent," said Goff, PhD, of the University of California, Los Angeles. This study was published online in APA's Journal of Personality and Social Psychology®.[2]

According to the study, researchers tested 176 police officers, mostly White males, average age 37 in large urban areas, to determine their levels of two distinct types of bias: prejudice and unconscious dehumanization of black people by comparing them to apes. To test for prejudice, researchers had officers complete a widely used psychological questionnaire with statements such as "It is likely that Blacks will bring violence to neighborhoods when they move in." To determine officers' dehumanization of Blacks, the researchers gave them a psychological task in which they paired Blacks and Whites with large cats, such as lions, or with apes.

Researchers reviewed police officers' personnel records to determine use of force while on duty and found that those who dehumanized Blacks were more likely to have used force against a Black child in custody than officers who did not dehumanize Blacks. The study described use of force as takedown or wrist lock; kicking or punching; striking with a blunt object; using a police dog, restraints or hobbling; or using tear gas, electric shock or killing. According to the study, only dehumanization was linked to violent encounters with Black children in custody; not police officers' prejudice against Blacks, whether conscious or not.

The authors noted that police officers' unconscious dehumanization of Blacks could have been the result of negative interactions with Black children. "We found evidence that overestimating age and culpability based on racial differences was linked to dehumanizing stereotypes, but future research should try to clarify the relationship between dehumanization and racial disparities in police use of force," Goff said.

"The evidence shows that perceptions of the essential nature of children can be affected by race, and for black children, this can mean they lose the protection afforded by assumed childhood innocence well before they become adults," said co-author Matthew Jackson, PhD, also of UCLA. "With the average age overestimation for Black boys exceeding four-and-a-half years, in some cases, Black children may be viewed as adults even when they are just 13-years-old." [1]

Cases in Point

- In his testimony to the grand jury, 28-year-old Ferguson police officer Darren Wilson described Michael Brown, the unarmed teenager he shot and killed, as an almost supernatural predator whose uncanny strength put the officer at mortal risk. Brown looked "like a demon" during their encounter, Wilson testified. "When I grabbed him the only way I can describe it is I felt like a five-year-old holding onto Hulk Hogan...that's just how big he felt and how small I felt just from grasping his arm." Officer Wilson is six feet, four inches tall, and weighs 210 pounds.[2]

- A witness called 911 on November 22 to report "a guy with a pistol" and although the weapon was "probably" fake, people were frightened. Cleveland Police Officer Timothy Loehmann fired the fatal shots at Tamir Rice within two seconds of arriving outside a recreation center where the sixth-grader was playing with a pellet gun. Video of the incident shows two police officers pulling up on the snowy grass near a gazebo where Tamir stood. Within two seconds of exiting the police car, Loehmann shoots the 12-year-old. In the video, neither Loehmann nor Garmback appear to provide medical assistance to Tamir, and Police Chief Calvin Williams said Tamir did not receive first aid until an FBI agent arrived on the scene four minutes later.

- Chicago Police Officer Jason Van Dyke, who has been the target of several complaints accusing him of excessive force and making racial slurs, was on paid desk duty. Van Dyke, 37, shot 17-year-old Laquan McDonald 16 times while he was 12 to 15 feet away, according to the Chicago Tribune.[3]

1 "The Essence of Innocence: Consequences of Dehumanizing Black Children," Journal of Personality and Social Psychology, published online Feb. 24, 2014; Phillip Atiba Goff, PhD, and Matthew Christian Jackson, PhD; University of California, Los Angeles; Brooke Allison, PhD, and Lewis Di Leone, PhD, National Center for Post-Traumatic Stress Disorder, Boston; Carmen Marie Culotta, PhD, Pennsylvania State University; and Natalie Ann DiTomasso, JD, University of Pennsylvania.

2 "Case: State of Missouri v Darren Wilson." (n.d.)

3 Kirkos, Bill. "Chicago Prepares for Laquan McDonald Video Release - CNN Video." CNN. Accessed December 12, 2015.

Interesting STOP Stories

I spoke to a mother, Nicole McGill, about STOP. She told me she instructed her son to: "Follow my instructions! Do not disrespect a police officer for any reason. Do not think, for any second, that you can do anything to put an officer in check. As a child, you are not in a position to challenge a police officer even if he is out of order. Police aren't trained to fear you."

Essentially, she has informed her son to allow her to fight for him. If he brings the information to her, she will be in a much better position to follow-up legally; however, her son needs to give her the ability to fight on his behalf by being respectful and following the police's orders.

Like this loving mom, my desire is always a better future for you. Therefore, I would never intentionally offer you advice that I think will cause you harm in any way. You have my word.

I asked a good friend of mine, Willard Hart, to read my book and provide feedback. After his positive feedback, he shared the following story with me:

"Dwayne! This book took me back down memory lane when I was a shorty living in Liberty City (Miami). One day, a friend of mine and I were minding our own business walking down the street with a small boom box playing Run DMC (Sucker MC's). We saw a police car speeding by us. Then all of a sudden, the car did a three-point turn heading back in our direction. My friend said, I think they are coming for us. Should we run?"

Willard, an honor roll student, asked his friend, "Why should we run? We haven't done anything wrong." Before the boys could contemplate a plan of action, the squad car was upon them. Willard stated the police called them over to the car and told them to get in. The boys, feeling afraid and uncertain, got in the back of the squad car. Willard asked, "Why are we in the back of your police car?"

The officer replied, "We just got a call about a burglary and you two fit the description."

As the officers pulled up to a house, a woman they recognized came out of the house, looked into the back seat and began cursing irately. He remembered the woman saying, "Why in the _____ do you have these two boys in your _____ car? I told 911 there were two MEN who tried to break into my house! I know these two boys! They are good boys! Get their _____ out of your car and go find the real _____ _____ criminals!"

Willard and his friend were 14-years-old at the time. Did these officers really mistake them for adults? Is it possible that a trained professional's judgment could be that far off? Is it a matter of training? Is it a racial bias or just plain unprofessionalism that does not deserve the right to wear a badge, nor uniform? These are the type of incidents that create deep mistrust between police and community.

Parents & Young People:

This is a great time to discuss the importance of respecting other people's property with your children. Although a child may not look at the situation as stealing, it is important to have that conversation with them. My brother and I thought we were "borrowing" the bikes until we returned them; however, the owner of the bike did not see it that way.

This might also be a good time to discuss consequences. Not all outcomes are bad. Perhaps if my brother and I were disrespectful to the officer or chose not to stop, the outcome may have been very different. Many students have disclosed to me that their parents told them, "If someone doesn't respect you, you don't have to respect them." Though I know you love your children, that advice is not sound advice. I teach my students they must respect authority even if they disagree with it. You have to teach your children that respecting authority is the right thing to do, especially during an encounter with the police. If you need to take further action, you can determine the best course of action once they arrive home safely. Often times our children take on the attitudes and values of their parents. Be mindful of your actions and conversations. Your children are always listening.

Law Enforcement:

Often times, young people make silly decisions and do not fully think through their actions. I understand that when you are called to a scene, it is not to babysit, parent or counsel. Your training is enforcing the law. I also know, sometimes, police discretion is more important than enforcing the law. In this case, if my brother and I had gone into the juvenile "justice" system (aka: juvie), I am not sure what kind of toll that would have taken on us or if the outcome would have disrupted our family. How would that decision have impacted our academics? Would teachers view us differently if we were placed into the system? Would it have shamed our mother or affected her job? Would we somehow become hardened and repeat offenders? Would our innocence disappear from being handcuffed, placed in the back of a squad car, fingerprinted and issued a case? In that moment, our entire lives could have changed dramatically.

Research states when a child experiences incarceration at a young age, they are more likely to get into more trouble. In the future, I am asking you to please consider the statistics in this book. If you are among the officers who unconsciously "dehumanize" black children, please remember this chapter.

Our young people need a fair chance to grow and become productive citizens. We need your help in this endeavor. Although my first encounter with law enforcement had a good outcome, the moment frightened us and could have gone in a completely different direction. I am happy my mother had the skills to advocate for her boys in a respectful manner.

Do you have a better understanding of the role everyone at The STOP has to play? The police officer alone did not determine the outcome. My brother and I along with our mother also played a vital role. We helped to determine the final outcome.

Discussion Questions

Young People:

- How can you help your parents fight for your rights?

- How do you think life would have changed if my brother and I were arrested for stealing bicycles? How could this outcome impact us in the long run?

- How did my mother, brother and I show respect for authority?

- What could have happened if Willard and his friend decided to run from the police?

- How would you define stealing?

- What do you think of Nicole McGill's advice to her son?

Parents:

- Have you spoken with your child about your expectations when encountering law enforcement?

- Have you informed your children to respect authority even if that respect is not given in return?

- What are your conversations in your home about law enforcement?

Law Enforcement:

- What can you do as a law enforcement officer / peace officer to ensure quality relations within the community?

- Do you think it is necessary to live within a community in order to effectively serve that community?

- Did our mother's demeanor have anything to do with us not being arrested? Do you think the outcome would be different if she showed disrespect and rudeness to the police officer?

- What do you think about the officer's decision not to arrest us?

Chapter 2
My 2nd Encounter: Officer "Bull" Bryant

The only picture I have with my father until adulthood.
Soon after this picture was taken, he and mom divorced.

I bullied kids in elementary school. I remember being angry because I always wanted my mother and father to reconcile. When I asked, "Momma, why can't you and dad get back together?" she never responded with an answer I wanted to hear. I wanted my dad to live with us. I wanted him to show up. I remember times when my mother asked us if we wanted to go to the mall with her. Many times, I decided to stay home because I just knew *this* was the day dad would come for me and return home. Every time I heard a car, I ran to the window and looked out to see if the car belonged to him, but it never did. When mom returned in the evening with my siblings only to find me in my room with the door closed, my sister laughed and said, "Boy you are so stupid! That man ain't coming for you!"

When the realization of my sister's words hit me, I clenched my fist in anger. Anger because every time a car drove by I rushed to the window. Anger because my brother and sisters were having fun and I was still at home. Sitting. Waiting. Looking for a man who wasn't coming. I felt abandoned. I had been lied to again. I felt angry because my "hero" never showed up.

My anger then turned inward. I was angry at myself because I was stupid enough to keep believing. As a child, I spent a lot of time frowning. I frowned so much that even to this day, when I'm thinking, it looks like I am frowning. My mother warned me that I would have a permanent frown if I didn't learn how to smile.

As I packed my book bag for school, I somehow packed my rage as well. The next day, someone was going to pay for his absence.

I shared my hurt and disappointment in the most inappropriate way. I fought because I did not know how to release my pain constructively. I believed in equal opportunity even at that age, so I equally beat up the black and the white kids. I also believed in affirmative action, so I affirmed my actions across the heads of other students. I hated to lose at anything. There was a guy named Doug W. who laughed at me after I lost a kickball game. I hit him so hard in his mouth that his teeth bit through his tongue (I'm not running for President, so I'm ok with you checking my references).

Due to my disruptive behavior, I got into a lot of trouble with my mom and school. On occasion, I prayed to God and asked him to, "Please let me go one week without getting a whooping or a paddling." After about a year, I knew God was real, because I went one whole week without one!

In my head, my father remained my hero even though there was NO tangible evidence that he cared anything about me. He lived less than 20 minutes away, yet he never showed up. Despite his absence, I decided to search for my father. I wanted to feel his love for me. In my mind, I knew he cared for me, but I just thought my mother did not want me to know it.

After having an argument with my sister when I was about 15-years-old, my mother made the statement, "I am the only grown person living in this home. If anyone else thinks they are grown, they can get out of my house because two grown people can't live here!" When I felt as though I could no longer live under such strict rules and regulations, I made a decision to move out of my mother's house.

Yep! At 15, I figured "a man's gotta do what a man's gotta do." Later that week when my mom left the house with my siblings, I chose to remain behind. I packed my bags and went to live with my father who was (guess what) a police officer. His nickname was "Bull" Bryant — a name given to him because he never had a problem going upside someone's head with his billy club. As stated earlier, my dad lived less than 20 minutes away from us, yet he never found time to visit. My mom later shared that although he was very charismatic he had a quick temper. Sometimes he couldn't control his temper. Mom shared an incident where a man was smart mouthing my dad and he beat him with his billy club until he was bloody. My mom became afraid after that encounter. They later divorced because of domestic violence.

Dad (aka James) worked for a small town police department called Eatonville Police Department. Eatonville, Florida was a proud town. It is the oldest Black incorporated town in North America. We lived there with our grandmother for a few years. Some people teased a few of Eatonville's police officers and did not take them seriously. Officer Polk was an obese officer who wore his belt like Barney Fife on the Andy Griffith Show. I also remember Chief Abney. He was a tall, kind professional man. He always wore his uniform with great pride. Chief Abney was both an officer and a gentleman.

Officer James Bryant
(aka: Dad)

The entire force had less than seven officers. Sometimes the community mocked some of the officers and said remarks like, "You're not a real police officer."

That didn't happen to my dad; he did not play that. Although he liked to joke around, he transformed into a new person when he put on his uniform. His shirt always ironed and tucked into his pants. Belt placed high above his waist. Hair properly groomed, and his shoes always shined. He sported a watch on his left wrist and a ring on the right hand. It wasn't a bird or a plane ya'll. It was Bull Bryant.

Interestingly enough, though he was dedicated and serious on his job, he was a terrible husband and father, leaving my mom to fend for herself with six children. For the few months I lived with him, I remember how he shined his bullets and polished his belt and shoes – I mean a spit shine. He stood in the mirror and gazed at himself with great pride.

Although my dad sometimes used excessive force on the job, he was not abusive toward me during my short stay. I guess he did the best he could in lieu of his limited parenting skills. For the majority of children, their first encounter with authority is their relationship with their parents. It so happened that my father, who was an absentee father, allowed me to gain another perspective of law enforcement.

In contrast, while living with him, I saw his authority came from his badge and uniform, and not who he was as a person. Could his excessive use of force have emanated from his lack of self-worth or the lack of contribution to his own family? My personal encounter with my father allowed me to see police officers from an entirely different perspective. Fortunately, I had other police officers that I looked up to as role models.

On the other hand, when I lived with my mom, we had full meals. We ate together as a family and engaged in family discussions. Mom was serious about our grades; she ensured we completed homework and got involved in school activities. She spoke with our teachers, making certain that we kept up academically.

Mom was strict...sometimes too strict. I remember when some of our friends' parents allowed them to spend the night at each other's houses. We thought that was cool so one day we asked if we could stay the night at a friend's house. My mother said, "If you want to have a sleepover, you and your brother can take your pillow in your sister's room and sleep over there. That will be your slumber party." Can you believe that?!

Dad wasn't strict at all. While living with my father, I ate pizza almost every night unless he took me over to one of his girlfriend's homes. They were very nice to me. They said I looked just like my father, so they called me "Lil' James."

In his neighborhood, I saw kids doing things my mother never allowed us to do in her home. My peers played basketball into the evening and no one did their homework. My dad wasn't home most of the time. My friends could play Atari, unlimited Pac Man and Asteroids!

I do not recall a single time when my dad asked me about my school or my education. He never asked me if I had a girlfriend or anything. He never reviewed my homework or knew my GPA. He just dropped off Domino's pizza and went to another assignment, leaving me to take care of myself. After sitting in the house alone, I wanted to get out and play with my friends. Some of the kids in his neighborhood cursed. I thought that was fun because I never let those words slip out of my mouth living with my mother. Though I was smart, school didn't seem as cool while living with my dad. Even as a child, I knew the surrounding environment around my dad's home would not allow me to become the man I dreamed of becoming. I knew this was not my home.

I also knew I didn't want to be like him. I finally saw firsthand what life was really like while living with dad. The fantasy ended. The bubble shattered. The hero I so carefully constructed within my head was nothing like I imagined. I had to leave his place, but I didn't want to return to my mother's super strict rules and regulations.

Dwayne's Note: If you are hurting because of an absent parent, try to speak openly to the parent you live with or a teacher, counselor, social worker or a trusted adult. The person should be someone who will allow you to share your feelings confidentially. However, remember, parents are really doing the best they can with what they have. Most can only teach you what they know and if they don't know it, they can't teach you. I learned from my experience with my father. The fantasy is always better than the reality. We can't live in a fantasy. We have to live in reality. Even if your reality is not great, determine this message within yourself: You will not engage in self-destructive behavior (drugs, alcohol, cutting, gangs and sex). Decide to work hard in school so you can give yourself a fair chance to graduate college or military and live a better life than what you may be living right now.

At the age of 15, I decided that I would be successful. I told myself that I would not drink alcohol. I would not take drugs. I would not join a gang. Instead, I will graduate from college. I will not have children and not take care of them. I will honor my word. I will make my mother proud. And to this date, I have stayed true to my word.

After realizing I would never develop into the man I desired to become while living with my dad, I packed my belongings and moved in with my godparents within a couple of months. They were a middle class couple, a retired military man and a nurse. At last, I finally found the love of a mother and father I had been searching for. They encouraged me to do well academically. Mr. Williams encouraged me to attend West Point because of his military background. I could actually hear my thoughts clearly in their stable and peaceful home, which was void of any arguing and cursing. They held hands and smiled — true love at its best. When my godfather said something sarcastic in his deep baritone voice, Mrs. Williams would say, "Oh Walter... that's not nice." The environment was a definite contrast from my previous living experiences.

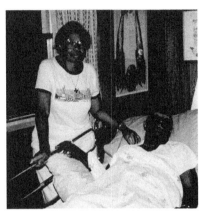

Unfortunately, I discovered that my godfather was dying. I remember crying as a boy because the family I had searched for and finally found was ending. I was a good boy – smart, hardworking and willing to do all the chores. Nevertheless, I had become more of a burden than I realized. Mr. Williams knew he was dying, and he did not want to put any additional stress on his wife.

One day, my godfather had a man-to-man conversation with me, one that I will never forget. After a few months of living there, he told me I needed to apologize to my mother. "Be a man and apologize for leaving, accept the punishment and go back home, son." I loved him dearly and obeyed his command.

That experience let me realize the truth behind Alfred Lord Tennyson's statement, "Tis better to have loved and lost than never to have loved at all." I had finally felt the love of a mother and father for which I had searched and longed. My brief encounter with the Williams showed me that love. Although he was dying, he promised me he would stay to see me graduate. It was a sad moment. I slowly packed my belongings with tears in my eyes and returned home. The love I felt at the Williams' home would last a lifetime.

Upon my return to my mother's house, I was determined not to give her any more problems. I began to excel academically. I had a world history teacher named Barbara Bey. She highlighted the African contributions to the planet, and I learned the builders of the pyramid looked like me. "King Tut was a Black boy just like you," she would say. The first university was in Africa

– Timbuktu. Science, astrology and mathematics all began in Africa! The Greek thinkers learned from Africans. This knowledge opened my mind, and it would never close again. I understood with great certainty that if my ancestors were kings, then I didn't have to act like a slave.

Instinctively, I knew a King does not behave like a slave and a slave does not act like a King. I chose to be a King. After Mrs. Bey's class, I never fought again. I never made anything lower than a B+ until college. I maintained excellent grades and never got into any trouble. From that moment, I began to smile. It seemed like I loved smiling. I remember some of my peers would ask, "Why do you smile so much?". Mrs Bey would tell them to "Leave him alone! You'd rather him smile than kick your tail."

Having this knowledge allowed my self-esteem and self-worth to increase. I began to respect my peers, my teachers and myself. I no longer felt inferior because I finally learned about the knowledge of self and the true history of my ancestors.

I finally understood how hard my mother worked to make ends meet. Her hard work was more than admirable. I learned many lessons from my mother that I enjoy today: a strong work ethic, self-love, love of history, love for community, determination, perseverance, grit, value for education and integrity, and the ability to smile beautifully and maintain a winning attitude!

I can't imagine being a single parent mother with six children and working two to three jobs. Many people would have experienced a nervous breakdown, but not Martha! I had a greater appreciation for her realizing that SHE was the hero, even when she got on my nerves. I also realized that having one loving parent in the home was better than living in a home where the mother and father didn't get along.

About two years ago, I had a conversation with a friend, MB, from high school. She had a mother and father in her home. I told her, I wish I grew up in a home like hers with a mother and a father. She said, "DB, you didn't want my home. Although I had a mother and father in the home, my father was an alcoholic. My home was always chaotic. Some days, I wish I wasn't even there." Wow! Who knew? That's why you just have to make the best out of any situation in which you are born.

My lesson for you: You can't choose your family; however, you can choose to remain positive and use your upbringing to make you a better person. Although I had created a fantasy in my head about a loving mother and father, that was not my reality. In retrospect, having a powerful loving mother or a loving father is better than having both parents in the home without love.

I must admit I have met some parents who were bad parents and should not have ever had a child. If you are in that home, then you will have to dig deep within yourself and determine this today: You will become successful. You will have good character. You will make this world a better place. No questions. No excuses. Life is tough, but failure can never be an option.

Although I didn't give my mom any more trouble, I made sure I was rarely home. I attended school all day. I had an internship with the State's Attorney's Office during my senior year. In addition, I served as an officer in the National Honor Society, belonged to the Spanish Honor Society and Social Studies Honor Society and became the first African-American President of the Florida State Spanish Conference. I also played in the marching band and worked at Taco Tico in order to contribute financially to my home. When I finally got home, I finished my homework, went to bed and started the day all over again.

I attended one of the top schools in Central Florida, Winter Park High, maintained a 3.6 GPA and graduated with honors. I also interned in Washington, D.C. with Congressman Bill McCollum.

Prior to writing this book, I never thought about the hard work and dedication I put into school. Often times, I tell my students, the best indicator of future success is past success. Though I am considered successful, sometimes I still wonder how my life would have turned out if I had a caring father to lighten my mother's load or someone to teach me the ways of manhood. Despite my circumstances, I didn't make excuses. I had to endure in order to earn the right to write this book with power and conviction.

Winter Park remains an affluent area with many "privileged kids." Was the playing field level? Did I have the same opportunities as my peers? Knowing what I know now, the answer is no; however, the great equalizer was having an awesome mother who valued education and stayed on top of us.

Whatever we started, mom made us finish. I wanted to drop out of the marching band because of all of my other responsibilities. She said, "No, if you quit things now because they are too difficult, when you become a man you will quit, and then you will walk out on your family. I'm not raising you to be that kind of man."

My brother and I were acolytes at Good Shepherd Church. We wanted to stop serving. She said, "No, when you make a commitment to God, you need to honor it." We didn't catch many breaks with her. When our friends were out playing on the weekends, we had to work by cutting yards and helping her man-friend with his rental properties. We worked ALL day to earn a Big Mac, large order of fries and a milkshake. Child labor was real in our home. Looking back, perhaps I was too busy with my academics, school activities and work that I didn't have idle time to be involved with law enforcement.

Toward the end of my senior year, my mother's voice got on my last nerve! She became overbearing. I think she feared raising lazy, trifling Black men. She saw no value in that as she had witnessed this scenario many times with the men in her life. I remember how she woke us up early with banging on the door on some Saturday mornings.

"It's time to wake up. Men don't sleep all day. Get up and get to work. Find some work," she told us. WHAT? I thought my mom had lost her mind. I knew I had to get out of that house, but this time I would not return. I would have gone to China if they offered a full scholarship.

My mom told all of her children, "At the age of 18, everyone is grown. Can't no grown people live in my house. You got three options:

1. You can go to college. If you go to college, I'm not paying a dime so that's why you better get some scholarships. You have four years of high school. That's your job. (I guess she forgot I had another job).

2. You can go to the military. If you go there, Uncle Sam will take care of you, but you are still getting out of my house.

3. You can get a job. If you get a job that means you can afford your own place, which means: You are still getting out of my house. Everythang is moving out at 18!"

At last, the end of my senior year finally arrived. It was time to graduate. Of roughly 780 graduating seniors, I was amongst the top 15%. I received a full academic scholarship. Winter Park High School had prepared me for college, and I was ready! Interestingly enough, I invited my father to attend my graduation even though he wasn't deserving of the opportunity. I just wanted him to be there.

He showed up sporting a red coat with white shoes. He really thought he looked sharp, but he looked like a clown to me. He walked very proudly as if he had something to do with my success. The only thing he contributed was genetics and two months of pizza. SMH.

Immediately after my high school graduation, while all of my peers celebrated, I rushed to my Godfather's bedside to show him my gown, honor scroll and diploma. Beaming from excitement, we held hands and he gave me a big smile. Then he placed one hand on top of mine and just nodded his approval. I felt so proud at that moment. He kept his promise to stay alive until I graduated. Shortly thereafter, he took his last breath and left us to cherish many wonderful memories.

The greatest university known to mankind, Florida International University, provided the full-ride academic scholarship. I was ready to go. Graduating high school felt exciting and scary. On autopilot, I packed my bags and drove to Miami with my mom and sister, Maria. Within days of being away, I became so thankful for my mother's parenting skills. It is the foundation for the man I am today.

I didn't appreciate my mother's strict rules until I went away to college. I later realized my mother's strictness was the best thing for us. I had values, morals and a sense of discipline and respect that some of my college peers lacked.

In retrospect, parents please remain strict. Keep the standards high. Set the expectations, and do not deviate even if your children complain and your family suggests you relax a bit. (I'm not talking about beating the stuffing out of your children or belittling them and calling that discipline because that isn't discipline. That is abuse. Remember, discipline without instruction leads to rebellion.)

"Train up a child in the way they should go and when they are old, they will not depart far from it." Proverbs 22:6

Reflections

My father found great pride in his uniform. He gained his nickname because of his use of force on the job. I wonder if that was the only way that he maintained control and power. Since he abandoned his wife and children, did he somehow find manhood in his uniform? I sincerely hoped he gave others the benefit of the doubt and did not use excessive force. I pray he used his power with respect and care.

As a husband, he left his wife and did not pay child support until my mother took him to court. Perhaps things were rough in his personal life, which is why he took such great pride in his authority. Maybe that explains why he demanded respect on his job because he had not earned much respect in his personal life. This will remain a mystery. I will have to believe he did the best he could with what he had. Prior to his death, I flew him here to Chicago for a weekend. I thought it was a necessary part of my journey as a man.

After resigning from my sales career with Johnson & Johnson (J&J), I decided to give him a call. He told me he had a heart attack and a stroke. He was on dialysis and in need of a kidney. After I hung up the phone, I cried like a baby. I cried because I knew very little about this man who, genetically speaking, was my father. He was dying and I could not recall a quality weekend with him.

I called him back and said, "Dad, I realize I don't even know much about you and you don't know me. I didn't know you had a heart attack and you didn't know I resigned from J&J almost two years ago. Dad, I am a good man. I have been on the Oprah Winfrey show three times. I mentor students throughout Chicago. I started my own business and I employ other people. Can we spend a quality weekend together."

He said, "Well son, let me call my doctor and see what he says." I just knew he was looking for a way out just as he had done in the past. It disappointed me, but I gave him an out. Surprisingly he called back and said, "Son, I'm coming to see you." I felt overjoyed. At last – my father was coming for me! I booked his ticket, put together an amazing itinerary and FedEx'd it to him.

Dad at Harpo Studios

When he first arrived, the electricity went out in my downtown building for some strange reason, so we had to walk up 15 flights of stairs. On the third flight, he began breathing heavily and holding his chest. I was scared. I didn't want him to die like that. We went up the stairs together, taking one step at a time. I always wanted to be close to my father. Helping him walk up the flights of stairs was not how I imagined it. Life is interesting.

We toured Chicago by car and train. Harpo Studios was our first stop. My friend, Candi Carter (now Executive Producer for The View), greeted him and gave him a tour of Harpo. He walked around the studio like a proud peacock. I received an award for speaking that weekend. At the event, people told him, "You must be proud of your son. We can see the apple doesn't fall too far from the tree." He laughed and smiled all night.

Before his departure, we found points of agreement. I had the opportunity to have a real conversation with him to ask him specific questions, such as "Why did you leave us?" "Why did you never come for us?" "Dad, I waited many times for you, thanks for finally showing up."

He looked at me and said, "Son, my doctor told me not to come. He told me that with my diabetes, this trip could be fatal. Finding a dialysis center and getting treatment could be too much stress on me." The doctor was right. The trip placed a lot of stress on him.

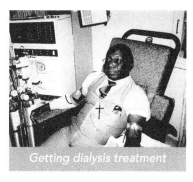
Getting dialysis treatment

Concerned for his health, I asked him why he made the trip.

"Dad, you almost died in the stairwell, and you look like death now. Why did you come here?"

Looking lifeless, he slowly raised his head, looked directly at me and said, "Son, I told my doctor, for all of my life I've never been there for my son. He has asked me to visit with him. I cannot let him down again. Even if this trip kills me, I am going to go and be with my son."

Those words felt like warm cleansing water to my soul. I never heard something so powerful and beautiful. We cried together, and for the first time in my life, we held each other. At that very moment, I forgave him. I no longer held his transgressions against him. I became free from anger. I no longer had that daddy pain – that feeling of not being good enough. At last, my daddy had come for me and given me the love I had searched for all my life. The absence of it became the source of so much pain and frustration throughout my life. In the twinkling of an eye, I felt whole.

My daddy told me he loved me. As we cried together, I asked him to bless me. "Would you please pray for me, just as Jacob blessed Joseph?" After his prayer, God allowed my heart to forgive him. At last, I was able to "exhale".

Although my father wasn't in my home growing up, he still taught me valuable lessons. I do know that because my father didn't keep his word, I learned the value of keeping mine. Because my father had children from multiple women, I knew I would have none unless I was married to their mother.

I remember one day when I spoke with my college mother, Director of Minority Student Services, Ozzie Ritchey. I said, "Mrs. Ritchey, I wish I grew up with a father because I think I would be better off." Mrs. Ritchey took my hands, looked me directly into my eyes and said in her soft, loving voice, "Son, I am so glad your father wasn't in the home with you."

"Mrs. Ritchey, why would you say something like that?" I asked.
In her great wisdom, she said, "My Dwayne, if your father was in the home with you, you wouldn't be exactly the way you are. I am so thankful to God that you are just the way you are."

Somehow, Mrs. Ritchey always knew how to calm my spirit.

Is it possible that healing my relationship with my father, a police officer, connects to my desire to help heal the relationship between police and community? Only God would have such wisdom and foresight. Living with my dad showed me another perspective of a police officer. Police are human beings. They make mistakes. They have personal pains, insecurities and struggles like the rest of us. My hope is that when a police officer puts on his/her uniform, they will act in a professional manner at all times, regardless of the issues they may struggle with in their personal or professional life. I hope that when we encounter a police officer, we will understand they are trained professionals and considered authority. Even if we do not like the person, we should respect the position and the authority behind the position. If we remember we are all human beings with similar goals and desires, being respectful in The STOP will become routine.

There are no coincidences. I realized the love that I longed for and the father I needed had been with me all along. My Heavenly Father had been by my side the entire time. My wonderful mother provided love, discipline and direction. May my earthly father rest in peace.

> **Dwayne's Note:** Mothers, if you and your children's father are no longer together, please do not speak negatively about him. I promise you, your child will discover that truth in time. When you speak negatively about the other person, it only creates anger and discontent within your child. Forgiveness is a powerful tool. It is not just for your child; it is for you as well.

Parents:

- What are your children's goals in life?

- How can you help them discover their purpose?

- Ask your child the following: "At what age do you become success-ful?" Let them know success starts **right now**! Encourage them to develop a plan with you today.

- How do you help your children manage their time?

- Have you shared Vision Boarding with your child?

- What would your child say about your parenting skills?

- Do you teach your child his/her heritage? Where are your people from?

- What are you doing to build your child's self-esteem / self-worth?

- If you are divorced, do you know the impact your divorce is having on your child?

- If you are a product of divorce, have you opened your heart to for-giveness?

- Is there someone in your life in need of forgiveness? What would it take to forgive them?

Young People:

- When was the last time you told your parents you love them?

- Are you appreciative for their love or are you never satisfied?

- How can you improve your attitude to make your home a better place to live?

- What can you do to show your parents your appreciation for them?

- How are you managing your time?

- Does your family spend enough quality time together?

- What are your long-term and short-term goals?

- What are your strengths as a student?

- Are you a leader or follower? What is your evidence?

- Do you know your GPA?

- What kind of student are you? What can you do today to improve your academics?

- Do you have quality relationships with your peers and teachers?

- If your parents are divorced, do you show the parent whom you are living with that you love and care for them?

- What did you think about me sharing my story with my father? Can you relate?

Law Enforcement:

- Do you understand the importance of you being present within your home?

- I believe you see the ugly side of mankind. How do you remember the beauty?

- How much quality time do you spend with your family? Are you present?

- Do you think my father took extra pride in his uniform because he lacked something in his personal life?

- What can you do to help heal police / community relations?

- How do you deescalate a situation when a person has no respect for your authority?

Mrs. Barbara Bey

CONFERENCE TIME

You are encouraged to discuss your child's progress with his teacher.

FIRST PERIOD

Reading Level:

Comment: Dwayne knows how to improve his P.E. & Art behavior

SECOND PERIOD

Reading Level:

Comment: Dwayne still has too much temper + causes trouble with classmates.

THIRD PERIOD

Reading Level:

Comment: Trying harder.

FOURTH PERIOD

Reading Level: 3

Comment: Continue to work on your temper, Dwayne. Have fun this summer

---

Lake Sybellia Elementary School Report Card
Behavior needed improvement.

Chapter 3
My 3rd Encounter: Discover Your Power

I was a senior at Winter Park High School – a proud Wildcat. As I drove home one day after band practice in my little red Chevrolet Chevette, I saw one of my friends standing on the sidewalk waiting for the bus. I asked if he wanted a ride because he was headed in the same direction. As soon as he jumped into the car, we heard a siren and saw flashing lights. This was my first encounter with a police officer as a teenager.

Little red Chevette

I found myself engaging in the The STOP Challenge I discussed in the previous chapter. As the female officer pulled us over, I began to slow down and think. Then, I stopped and looked both ways—my past and future. First, I examined my past and thought to myself: I am an Honor Roll student at Winter Park High School. I am in the National Honor Society, I am liked by my peers and teachers. Then, I looked into my future: I am college bound. I will be the first in my family to graduate college. I have a bright future ahead of me. I also thought about the officer. Although I had a suspicion as to why she pulled me over, I was determined to be respectful during the encounter.

After looking both ways, I was confident that I had not broken any laws. I had no reason to fear nor was there a desire to be disrespectful. I felt annoyed by The STOP. I sincerely believed the officer stopped me because she saw a Black boy riding in the car alone and another one jumping into the car. I did not understand how our situation looked suspicious. We were just two teenagers coming home from school. We did not drink nor did we take or sell drugs. No gang involvement. We were good students (I was the smartest though ☺).

Although I did not understand why she stopped us, we both knew not to jump out of the car and start running. There were no drugs in my vehicle. Although I believed this stop was completely unjustified, I had a responsibility in The STOP. I had a role to play in the outcome.

"Do you know why I stopped you?" the officer asked.

"Officer, I have no clue why you stopped me. I was hoping you would tell me," I replied.

"She's stopping us because we are Black and she doesn't have anything else to do," my friend chimed in. Knowing things could go wrong quickly, I sharply told him to be quiet and to let me talk to the officer.

I knew very well that he was a visitor in my car, and it was my responsibility to make sure that neither of us did anything to cause unnecessary escalation. I also knew that his statement was correct; however, since we were stopped without a reason, I did not want things to go wrong. The officer never said why she stopped me. She did, however, ask for my driver's license. I gave her my license and waited patiently for her to return. I knew I had no criminal record with law enforcement.

While she ran my license, the conversation in the car turned heated. Though we both agreed the STOP was B.S., we had different opinions on how to respond to the situation. I knew if we started smart-mouthing the officer, she could call for backup. Who knows what may have transpired in that scenario.

I do not remember having a natural disdain for law enforcement. We were not harassed like some of the stories I heard from my students.

As the driver, it was my call to choose how we responded. I chose to answer the officer's questions. I let her know that we were students coming from school and I saw my friend in need of a ride. The officer went on to say, "Well watch your speed" and gave me a citation for speeding even though she stopped us just past a stop sign… in a Chevette. (I do not think the Chevette could speed even if I pressed the gas all the way down to the floor.)

Before leaving, I looked at her name badge to remember it. I knew that was not the day to challenge her and let her know that I was probably smarter than her. I just wanted to drop my friend off and get home safely.

When I got home, I discussed The STOP with mom. Our conversation ended after she warned me to be careful. I was still upset about The STOP. I thought, "Why is it fair that an officer can stop us for no reason. Why do I have to pay a ticket when I was not speeding! Why is this ok?"

Fortunately, at that time I participated in a work study program while in high school. Because I had enough credits to graduate and I maintained excellent grades, I started an internship with the State's Attorney's Office. I shared the story with one of the attorneys the day after The STOP, and he agreed the ticket was B.S.

The attorney told me that if I was his kid, he would be upset about The STOP. I asked him if he thought The STOP happened because we were Black (he was a White attorney), and he said, "It is possible, but I don't have enough evidence." He asked if the situation really bothered me. I said, "YES! I do not think it was fair. I'm an honor student at one of the top schools in Central Florida."

He then asked me one of the most important questions I have ever heard in my life.

"Tell me: do you want to just complain about it like most people do, or do you want to do something about it?"

I quickly responded, "I want to do something about it! But what can I do?"

He showed me that I could choose to pay the ticket or contest it in court with evidence and facts and challenge the officer in front of a judge. I didn't know I had recourse against the officer. I thought her word was the law. I began to understand the officer's word wasn't the final word. I chose to take action and developed a plan. I didn't want to become someone who complained about a police encounter but did not assert my power to affect change. I wanted the officer held accountable. I spoke to my mother about it, and she said, "Fight the case!"

I looked up the statute on the ticket. The ticket said I was speeding. I went back to the scene and took pictures of the stop sign. The Polaroid worked just fine at that time (parents, you may have to explain the Polaroid). I took pictures of my car at the stop sign and a picture of the exact spot we were stopped. I also showed the bus sign by the stop sign. I even went to the mechanic to bring in paperwork showing that my speedster was a 4-cylinder

Chevette.

I wore my best suit on the court date. My hands shook from nervousness. Here is a Black boy taking a White police officer to court, presenting in front of a White judge and another White city attorney. I was called into a room and asked if I wanted to take the case before the judge.

"Yes," I replied.

"On what grounds?"

"I was unfairly given a ticket, and I would like the judge to decide if it was just."

After receiving some assurances from the city's attorney that I would not win against the police, I decided to proceed anyway. I was not sure of the worst that could happen, but I did not think it would be worse than me not believing in myself and not doing the right thing when I had a chance.

Dwayne's Note: Young people, you have to be aware of your resources! You have teachers, parents and friends of your parents. Do not allow anger and frustration to boil inside. Use that frustration constructively to intelligently defend yourself. Make sure it is at the proper time, with respect, in the proper way.

Remember, your friends may not have enough wisdom to give you the best advice. Find intelligent adults who will help.

A loud voice called my name and my ticket number.

Laaawd, Jesus!!! Help me! Everything in me wanted to run out of the court room, but my mind guided my body. "Please raise your right hand…. Do you swear to tell the truth…?" After the long question, I answered, "Yes, your Honor, I promise. My mom told me to never swear."

The police officer stated her version of the story. It surprised me that she lied on the stand. I wanted to interrupt and say, "That's a lie! That's not what happened at all!" Somehow, I knew better. I breathed really hard to keep my peace. When the officer finished, it was my turn.

I told the judge, "With all due respect to the officer, her recollection of the events is not what happened at all." I stated the fact that I was driving down the street in my little red Chevette (I hope Prince does not get upset with that description).

"After stopping at the stop sign, my friend was waiting for the bus. He asked if he could have a ride. I told him to get in. As soon as he got in and I took off, the officer flashed us with her lights and we were stopped."

I showed the judge the pictures of the stop and the distance between the stop sign to where we were pulled over. I showed the judge my report card, student involvements, band membership and anything else I could find as a character reference. The judge knew, it was impossible to speed in the contraption we were in that day. The judge stated that, "Based on the evidence, this ticket is dismissed! You are free to go." The judge ruled in my favor. I WON! I WON!

This is why you must take your education seriously. I think my academic standing, my involvement at school, my character and my ability to advocate for myself were important factors in the judge's decision. The evidence didn't hurt either.

I won more than just a case that day. I won my pride. I won the right to be free. I won the freedom to know in my heart that I walked in truth. It seemed as if justice was possible. It seemed that if I was willing to do the work, I would not subject myself to dishonest police officers. That day shaped all of my encounters with law enforcement moving forward.

Something you should know when being pulled over:

The most likely reason people are stopped while driving is for violations of the vehicle code. The laws governing driving privileges consist of more than 100 pages. It is not uncommon for a driver to violate a code without knowing it. For example, vehicle code says that you must signal your intent to turn or change lanes 100 feet (10 car lengths) before doing so.

Other Reasons Individuals Are Stopped While Driving:

- Criminal investigations often involve officers looking for a suspect, a witness or a suspect's vehicle.

- Your vehicle may match the description of someone the officer is looking for or the suspect's vehicle.

The Providence External Review Authority developed a training manual, "Understanding Police Procedures If You Are Stopped by Police." In this manual, they recommend the following:[4]

Things to Do When Stopped

Officers are trained to place a great deal of emphasis on their safety and survival, so they can do their job of protecting others. Many of these guidelines are based on the safety procedures that officers follow.

- Slow down, safely pull over to your right when you can and make a complete stop.

- Please stay in your car with both hands in sight on the steering wheel, and wait for the officer to approach.

- Do not get out of the vehicle unless asked to do so.

- Show the officer your driver's license, vehicle registration and proof of insurance when instructed to do so.

- If stopped by a policeman at night, the first thing you must do is put your inside dome light on.

- If you do not agree with the reason for the citation, the reason for the stop or the officer's demeanor, keep track of all pertinent information about the stop, including the officer's name and identification number. Officers are unable to handle your complaint on the scene.

- If you do not agree with the reason you were arrested, you have a right to legal representation, and all sides of your case can be presented in court before a judge. This is why being respectful is always the right thing to do.

4 "Understanding Police Procedures If You Are Stopped by Police". (n.d.). Providence: Providence External Review Authority.

Interesting STOP Story.

In an effort to create a website for this book, I contacted Go Daddy to reserve a domain name. TheStop.com was already taken; however, they said it was for sale for $20,000! Can you believe that? Ain't nobody got $20K for a domain name. We got creative and reserved: TheStop4Teens.com,

TheStopStory.com and AboutTheStop.com.

As I continued to talk to Zach, the representative, about the book, he said, "You sound really excited. I can tell it's going to be great."

Then he went on to tell me about one time when he encountered The STOP. He was driving about 95 mph through a small town in Arizona with three of his buddies. When the officer pulled him over, his buddies started making smart comments in the back. The officer looked him directly in the eyes and said, "Listen to me. I'm going to say this one time. I want you to look each of your friends directly in the eye and tell them, right now, YOU have ALL of their lives in your hand. I would advise them to be quiet and understand that I will ONLY be talking to you."

Whoooooooa! I don't know what the officer meant by that comment, but Zach made sure that he took responsibility and control over all comments coming out of his car.

Young people, you have to remember that when you are driving, YOU control the car. Do not allow anyone in your car to disrespect the officer. Sometimes, our friends allow their ego to speak for them. I want you to always have your mind engaged. Tell them and their ego to SHUT UP!

According to PERA: Providence External Review Authority, as the driver, you are responsible for[5]:
- The conduct of the passenger. This covers such things as passengers throwing trash out the window, hanging their arms or legs out of the window or acting in a disorderly manner.
- Ensuring that all passengers wear their seat belts and that children are properly secured.

5 Aveni, T. The MMRMA Deadly Force Project: A Critical Analysis of Police Shootings under Ambiguous Circumstances (Spofford, NH: The Police Policy Studies Council, 2008), http://www.theppsc.org/Research/V3.MMRMA_Deadly_Force_Project.pdf

Young People & Parents:

I have said it many times, and I will say it again: when/if you have an encounter with law enforcement, you have a responsibility. That responsibility is to show respect at all times. If the officer is being disrespectful, do not give him/her a reason to escalate a situation. Remember The STOP Challenge. Your primary goal is to get home and determine your plan of action if it is necessary.

I am not telling you not to seek justice; I am telling you that there is a time and a place for everything. Remember, the officer has a boss and his boss has a boss and there are judges to determine whether or not justice has been served. Choose your battles wisely. In the example above, exchanging words with the officer would have caused me more harm than good. She could press one button on her radio and five squad cars could be on the scene. Are you understanding me?

There is a book called the Art of War written by Sun Tzu. The book is about military strategy. The premise of the book is simply: If you are in a fight and you do not know yourself, nor your enemy, you will lose the fight every time. If you are in a battle and you know yourself but you do not know your enemy, then you will only win the battle half the time. If you are in an all-out war and you know yourself AND your enemy, then you will be prepared to win the war ALL the time.

Let me be quick to say, I don't want you to think that the police are the enemy. That should never be the case. I do want you to better understand yourself and the police and their objectives so that if you have an encounter, you will be prepared to create a positive stop for everyone involved. I want you to be prepared to win in the encounter every time, even if winning means accepting the consequence because you were wrong during the encounter. Accepting when you are wrong also builds character and provides a road map for improvement.

When, and if, you are in a police encounter, teach yourself to:

Remain calm.
- This is your opportunity to look "right" into your future. What are your goals in life? What do you want to do? Are you going to college? Graduating from high school? Do you want to go to the prom? Do you have a boyfriend/girlfriend? Do you want to go home?

  Think of all the reasons you need to make this a good encounter. At the end of The STOP, what you want to do is go home. With the help of your parents at home, you can coordinate an intelligent response if necessary.

Keep your hands in plain sight.

- If you are in a car, place both hands on the steering wheel. If you are on the street, keep your hands out of your pocket. If you have something in your hands, open your hands so the officer can see the object clearly. Tell them what you are holding in your hand if necessary.

I was listening to NPR radio about fatal police shootings in Los Angeles. In all of the fatalities, police officers stated they thought they saw the subject reaching for a weapon. All were cleared of the shooting. This is why you must remove that assumption as a possibility. NEVER reach for ANYTHING before being instructed. If you are in your car, you may want to quickly pull your phone out to record the encounter. If you can't pull it out before the police officer approaches you, then leave the phone wherever it is.

Aron Weller, Trooper with the Indiana State Police stated, "First thing that comes to mind of course with every officer when they stop a vehicle is, does this person have a gun, is this person going to fight me today, is this going to be a good easy stop or is this going to be something that I have to use all my training that I've been taught?"

Often times, we do not consider the thoughts or apprehensions of the police officer during our encounter with them. Although he or she has been trained for The STOP, we should always be mindful that our words, tone and body language will also impact the encounter. The officer should be mindful of his/her tone, actions and body language as well. We must understand, both parties have a responsibility to ensure a positive outcome in the stop.

Dwayne's Note: Parents, Teachers, Youth Providers and Young People. I am providing an array of information for you in this book. Please pay close attention to the reference below:

The Police Policy Studies Council, an interdisciplinary, research-based, training and consultation corporation, conducted a Critical Analysis of Police Shootings Under Ambiguous Circumstances. The MMRMA Deadly Force Project. Thomas J. Aveni, MSFP stated the following in his Executive Summary, page 4: [5]

"Significant correlation does exist between officer action and action of the subject (shoot, surrender with object in-hand and surrender without object in-hand); acting quotient; and video setting (burglary, robbery and mugging). Also, significant correlation exists between an officer's action and two attributes of the subject: subject's age and subject's dress. Officers/deputies are more likely to shoot when the subject is young (rather than old), in punk dress (rather than business dress), and the acting quotient is high (rather than low).

Officers are also more likely to shoot in robbery scenarios than in muggings and more likely to shoot in mugging scenarios than in burglary scenarios. Lastly, officers are more likely to shoot when a subject's action is "shoot" rather than when a subject's action is "surrender without," and more likely to shoot when a subject's action is "surrender without" an object in-hand than when it is "surrender with an object in-hand." This apparent anomaly is explained by the high correlation found in scenarios, which had been assigned high "acting quotients" (AQ) for the amplitude of critical acting variables. The higher the acting quotient, the higher the correlation was for officers shooting "unarmed" suspects.

Officers aren't trained to fire a certain amount of bullets, according to Aveni. Court cases over the years have ruled that police can continue shooting until the suspect is no longer a threat to public safety.

His research shows that on average, an officer will fire two or more shots after they have received a visual cue that they should stop, based on the time it takes to "apply the brakes" of a neuromuscular response.

A 1994 U.S. Supreme Court case, Plakas v. Drinski, ruled that police are not required to use less lethal force (like pepper spray or a Taser) before resorting to deadly force (a gun) if there is a threat to someone's life. The law entrusts the decision of the level of force that is used to what the officer considers reasonable.

My beautiful, intelligent, awe-inspiring, bright young people (and your parents): Do you understand what I shared in the section above? You can dramatically increase your probability of being shot under certain circumstances, such as the following:

- Young (this is more than likely 10 – 24-year-old category. You can't change this right now)

- "In Punk dress" (rather than business dress). I think the subliminal word is: "Thug Dress" – long white T's, sagging pants, baggy sweats. (Be mindful, people judge you based on how you dress, just as you judge others)

- High-level Acting Quotient. This means you are moving rapidly or maybe in a threatening manner. Waving your arms could be considered "disrespectful actions." (Keep your hands visible. Calm your emotions, be mindful of your gestures.)

- Robbery scenarios

- When your actions say: Shoot vs. Surrender. (You can decide what that means)

- When your hand holds an object (Keep objects out of your hands during an encounter)

Personally, I've said many times after a police shooting: "They didn't have to shoot them that many times!" According to Aveni, court cases over the years have ruled that police can continue shooting until the subject is no longer a threat to public safety. I don't know about you, but this clearly says: Shoot to KILL. The law entrusts that the level of force used is what the officer considers reasonable.

From me to you: Please do not give the officer a reason to pull his firearm. They are not trained to shoot you in the leg, hand or foot. That is what we see in the Hollywood movies.

In a recent conversation with David Bursten, Captain – Chief Public Information Officer, Indiana State Police, I asked him if police officers were trained to Shoot to Kill? He explained the following:

Law enforcement is trained to shoot center of mass. The reason is, in a stress situation there is a loss of fine motor skill. Shooting at "center mass" or the trunk of the body increases the likeliness of striking anywhere from the hips to the upper chest and any area to the left or right. Aiming at center mass decreases the chance of missing and having the bullet strike an innocent bystander. It is correct we are trained to shoot until the threat is no longer present. That means the suspect makes true indications of surrendering after being shot, or is clearly incapacitated, or dies.

Answer the questions that are asked.

- I know sometimes police officers will ask you questions like: "Do you know why I stopped you?" "What are you doing in this neighborhood?" "Do you have any drugs or weapons on you?" "Are you a gang member?" "Whose car are you driving?" or maybe even, "How are you today?"

  Those questions could annoy you, especially if you live in the nice neighborhood he/she stopped you in and the nice car you are driving is yours or your parent's or if you do not take drugs at all, never been involved in a gang and do not own any weapons.

  Trust me! I know those kinds of questions, especially if you have done nothing wrong, can get on your nerves; however, my rules are not going to change. Whether respect is given to you or not, always be respectful when in an encounter with law enforcement.

- After having various conversations with law enforcement, those questions are very important to the officer's safety and your own. Many people would tell you to answer differently. Some would tell you to know your rights. Some people would tell you to quote the Constitution. I think you should always know your rights and learn the Constitution. However, the best time to begin quoting it is not during your encounter.

  So, while you are taking the time to learn your rights and quotes from the Constitution and The Amendments, answer the questions in a calm manner and keep sarcasm to a minimum. Remember, all those people offering you that great advice about The STOP usually will not be with you when The STOP actually occurs, so employ wisdom.

Don't get into an argument with the police officer.

- Again, I believe more than 90% of officers are good, decent people; however, that leaves 10% with questionable characters. These individuals will try to provoke you. They will try to work your nerves. They are not professional, so being disrespectful will not help you in any way. Remember, it is only a test to see if you will remember the discussion throughout this book. Stay focused on your future, not this present moment. Be respectful even if it is not returned. Do not stoop to their level. You have a parent(s)/guardian(s) waiting for you at home. Give them the ammunition to fight for you!

Don't even think about running or speeding away!

- Remember what I said earlier. When you are at The STOP, you need to look to your left and right, meaning look into your past and look toward future. Think about your frame of mind and the officer's.

- What happens if your past is shady? What if you were arrested or you are on probation? What if you do have drugs on you or a weapon or you are in a stolen car with a friend? Well, if that is the case, you need to be more mindful of your words and actions because the officer may already know your history with the law and already prejudged you.

  Running will not solve the issue, and most times, you will not get away. If you do not believe me, go to a race track. Give two people a radio, and place them on opposite ends of the track. Stand by one person with the radio. Get down on your mark. Get set. GO! Try to get to the other end of the track before that person can radio others and alert them that you are coming. Couldn't do it could you? And that is how silly it is trying to outrun the police officer.

They have radios and can call dozens of other officers quickly. Plus, his/her bullets will outrun you every time – I do not want you to test that one though. I am sure there are enough cases to prove my point. I want you to get to the place where you are always thinking. If you do have an illegal substance or weapon, just tell the officer what you have in your possession.

KEEP YOUR HANDS IN THE AIR!

Dwayne's Note: I am not advocating running from a police officer as I stated above. However, I just remembered the case where a late 20/early 30-something year old man ran from a police officer. The 60 plus year old officer caught him on foot. Why? Because the dude had his pants pulled down and couldn't run. How stupid does a grown man look walking with his pants pulled down and his underwear showing? Young folk, y'all don't look much better; your only excuse is young and trying to be cool. Men. Let's be men. We should be setting the trend, not following behind boys. When men stand up, boys will sit down. A gentleman wears his pants around his waist. There is no need to show your underwear. A belt is a beautiful and often times necessary accessory. Have pride in yourself. Pull your pants up.

Comply with the officer, even at the point of arrest… DO NOT RESIST.

- Okay, let's talk. Trust me when I tell you this is going to be difficult, especially if you are being wrongly accused or mishandled. Your first reaction will be to pull away or strike back or defend yourself. That would be my first reaction as well; however, many times that is where things go wrong.

- This is exactly what that 10% of officers with questionable traits want you to do. They want you to resist so they can add additional charges against you and maybe even rough you up a bit. In extreme cases, they may even desire to kill you. Yes, I said it! That is tough to think about, but I would rather you think about it now and plan a better response than not think about it and experience an outcome that is not to your liking. Trust me, your mother would rather visit you in jail than visit you at the funeral. Ya feel me?

- Here is something you should know. I participated in a firearms safety class, Conceal and Carry.

When I was taking the CCW class, the trainer stated:
- Do not pull your gun out unless you are prepared to shoot.
- Do not shoot unless you are prepared to kill.
- If you shoot, it is better that you are the only witness because dead men can't talk!

Can you believe that? I was shocked! In retrospect, with all of the incidents and deaths, someone else has apparently been trained in the same way. Do not give them a reason to pull their weapons – period.

- If they ask your name, state it.
- There should be a probable cause for any police officer to stop you or detain you. Even if you do not think you have done anything wrong, there still may be probable cause.

Interesting STOP Story:

Last week, I had breakfast with a well-known and respected former President of a college in Chicago. He shared an encounter that happened to him one day. He had just returned to Chicago from Mississippi. As he headed into a building for an appointment, he noticed several police cars outside. The officers approached him and asked for his name and what he was doing in the area.

He answered and asked them why the heavy police presence. They told him someone had just robbed a bank and he fit the description. (We ALL knew HE did not rob a bank; however, that was their "probable cause"). They asked him what he did for a living, and he told them he worked at a local college. They asked for his job title, and he said, "I am the President", to which one officer replied, "Yeah right."

I was bothered listening to the story. Why did he have to prove himself? Well…the fact of the matter was, he was being detained, and because they had probable cause, he had to prove himself and his identity. When the supervisor came to the scene, he was angry with the officers. The suspect was described as a Black male with glasses and 5 feet, 7 inches tall. My friend matched the description, except for the suspect's weight, which was about 220lbs. Whoa! Wait just one minute. My friend was clearly not over 150 pounds soaking wet.

The supervisor asked why in the "H-E- double toothpicks" were they detaining my friend instead of finding the real criminal! They released him immediately. This is another example of the 10% purposefully wasting someone's time for their enjoyment.

Do not give them the satisfaction of the reaction. I asked my friend if he filed a report. He said, "No." He was glad to teach them a lesson about false assumptions. Well, I disagree with that one.

Who knows how many times those officers have held someone up without a legitimate probable cause? Who knows how many times they may have falsely accused someone or racially profiled them? In my opinion, officers who misuse their power or purposely, and without merit, profile someone just to make them afraid, do not deserve to wear a uniform or carry a badge (and certainly not a gun).

- If you are being harassed, look for the officers' names on their badge and take note of their badge numbers. Remember it. Go and file a report. Do not tell the officer you are going to file a complaint during

The STOP. When the encounter is over, write down their information or put it in your phone. Citizens should not be afraid of police officers. We should always respect their authority; however, accepting unfair or unprofessional treatment is not acceptable.

- If they ask for your ID, provide it. (Hopefully you do not have anything to hide, and if you do, be honest because it will come out anyway.)

- If you are in a vehicle, you must provide your license, proof of insurance and registration. This is not the time to state your rights. Give up the ID and wait patiently.

Don't ask the officer a bunch of unnecessary questions like, "Do you know who my parents are? Don't you know I know my rights?" At this time, the only right I want you to have is the right to shut up and the right to be respectful. You do not have to prove your intelligence.

- Anything you say can and will be used against you in the court of law. Why give someone ammunition to use against you? Sit or stand quietly. Do not curse at the police. Do not threaten or provoke them. Use your head and not your ego.

- If a police officer asks to search your car, you have the right to refuse the search.

However, if the officer has probable cause, he/she can search your car. Not sure what defines probable cause? Let me explain it to you. Probable cause is a reasonable suspicion by law enforcers that a crime has been committed or that evidence of a crime will be located in a search, allowing law enforcers to make an arrest or conduct a search without a warrant.

For instance, you open the car and a cloud of weed blows out the window. You are probably smoking an illegal substance; that's probable cause (unless you have your "medicinal" paper-work or the laws in your state have changed regarding legalizing marijuana).

Dwayne's Note: First of all, you shouldn't be smoking weed anyway! Many people are out here selling synthetic weed and some silly people are smoking that mess! It is causing people to become violent; some are being rushed to the hospital and some people are

48

dying over it. It is bad business, and for what purpose? To get High?

A friend whom we shall refer to as AR shared that her 17-year-old brother had a few puffs of marijuana, which was laced with PCP. He had an immediate reaction and was rushed to the hospital. To this day, at the age of 22, he is being taken care of inside of a nursing home. Just imagine – a few puffs and you have blown the rest of your life. You must ask yourself, what is the value of your life?

I know life is tough, but when you smoke weed to escape your problems, they only get worse when you come off the high. Deal with your life; create the world you desire even if you are living in drama. Besides, the weed you guys are buying on the streets is laced with chemicals, which can cause you serious harm.

Let's get back to probable cause. If you are stopped and the officer hears someone from inside the trunk banging and screaming for help – probable cause. If you have a firearm on the seat, it could be probable cause (you must carry your conceal and carry license). If there is a big black plastic bag in the back seat with some red-like substance dripping from it – probable cause.

Without probable cause or a search warrant, the officer cannot legally search your vehicle or your body. If the officer asked can he/she search you, you have the right to refuse that as well. You can simply ask the officer, "Do you have a search warrant?" If they do, ask to see it. If they have it, gladly surrender to the officer for the search.

I'm not this smart. I learned this because a friend of mine, Louisa Nuckolls, is an Assistant State's Attorney. She shared information from the American Civil Liberties Union (ACLU), which states: [6]

- Lawfully, the Fourth Amendment protects citizens from unlawful searches by "prohibiting unreasonable searches and seizures (includes arrest) and requires any warrant to be judicially sanctioned and supported by probable cause." This law protects against arbitrary arrests, search warrants, stop-and-frisk, safety inspections, wiretaps and other forms of surveillance.

Amendment IV secures the right of people in their persons, houses and papers.

6 *Know your rights at a protest: ACLU of Pennsylvania (n.d.). Available at: http://www.aclu-pa.org/issues/freespeech/right-protest/know-your-rights-protest/*

Now, this can be tricky. Police officers KNOW the law and what they can and cannot do. They also know most of you do not know the law.

My concern here is the 90% wouldn't try to search you without the proper warrant or probable cause. The other 10% would try. Maybe they are suspicious of something. Maybe your behavior, clothing or smell could cause them to suspect drug use or gang affiliation. Maybe they are just racially profiling you. Maybe they just do not like someone who looks like you or sounds like you. (Hey, that is possible too!)

Just as they may be correct in their assumption, they also could be wrong. I would hate for you to have something planted on you. If you are dealing with the shady 10%, I would not trust their ethics. You will have a heck of a time trying to prove why they "found" what they discovered on you or inside your vehicle. It is important to know your rights.

According to the ACLU (American Civil Liberties Union), police may pat-down your clothing if they suspect you are carrying a weapon. Do not physically resist. Make it clear that you do not consent to further search.

Ask if you are under arrest. You have a legal right to know. Although you may be detained, it does not mean that you are under arrest.

Again, do not bad mouth the officer or use profanity or threatening words. If you are innocent and begin using such language, it could lead to an arrest.

If you are at home, police do not have the right to search your home without probable cause or a search warrant.

Remember, most police officers are good, law abiding professionals. They are not there to pick on you. Whether you like them or not, you should respect them. Showing signs of respect doesn't make you weak at all. Ultimately, resisting the urge to smart mouth an officer shows strength and intelligence.

Dwayne's Note: I spoke to my friend Louisa Nuckolls; she's an Assistant State's Attorney. She shared the following: The RIGHT to an attorney does not kick in until one is in a "custodial interrogation" situation. That's also the point where the police officer MUST give the person his Miranda Rights. Miranda is not required in a "non-custodial interrogation."

So, when is a person "in custody"? It depends upon several factors including, but not limited to: the time, location and duration of the encounter; the number of police officers present; whether the person was told that he was free to leave; and at least 10 additional factors. It should be noted that a person can be in custody while he's on the street, in his car or even in his own home—he doesn't have to be in a police station. It also should be noted that the courts balance out all of the relevant factors in making a determination of whether someone is in custody. One factor that is weighed heavily in once case may hardly be considered at all in another case—it REALLY all depends on the facts of the specific case!

A person who is being questioned for hours would generally be considered to be "in custody", so most courts would rule that questioning MUST cease once that person asks for an attorney.

CONSTITUTIONAL RIGHTS:

- If you are being questioned before an arrest, all persons (juveniles and adults) have the following rights to remain silent and also request the presence of an attorney.

- If you are being questioned *after* an arrest, all persons (juveniles and adults) have the following rights, referred to as Miranda Rights:

> *You have the right to remain silent. Anything you say can and will be used against you in a court of law. You have the right to talk to an attorney and have him or her present while you are being questioned. If you cannot afford to hire an attorney, one will be appointed to represent you at no expense.*

- Stay put and stay calm. Don't walk or run from police.
- Don't interfere with an officer making an arrest or a traffic stop.

RIGHTS OF POLICE:

- Police may use reasonable force to make an arrest or detain someone.
- If they have probable cause, they can search you, your vehicle and in some circumstances, your residence.
- If they have probable cause, they can seize your property.
- If they have reasonable suspicion that you have a weapon or illegal substance, they can search you.

Law Enforcement:

Please remember that you are most likely more knowledgeable of the law. Most citizens do not know the law or their rights. When someone tells you they know their rights or behaves rudely, I understand how it may annoy you and cause you to get frustrated and defensive.

When I spoke to Trooper Weller, he shared that Indiana State Police were trained in Verbal Judo. Basically, Verbal Judo is a simulation of someone using profanity and being rude to the officer. It allows them to experience rude behavior and offers them an opportunity to deescalate the situation during their training in hopes they will employ that training during a real life occurrence.

I know you are human and have feelings as well, but please remember that you are the only one trained for The STOP. Often times, young people do not think everything out. Sometimes they think they know more than what they actually do. After all, we were young people at some point as well.
If their behavior annoys you and causes aggravation, please exercise additional patience. Ask yourself, how would you want another officer treating your sons or daughters?

Students

- Being respectful to authority – is it a sign of weakness or strength?
- What is the best way to fight for your civil rights?
- Why is it important not to yell out in a courtroom?
- How would you feel about yourself if you allowed others to abuse the law at your expense?
- Why was it important for me to fight the speeding ticket? What did I gain? How do you think that impacted my self-esteem?
- How can you be proactive and respectful when encountering law enforcement?
- Whose responsibility is it to control your actions?
- Why is it important to be respectful to law enforcement, even if you feel you have not done anything wrong?
- Do you sag your pants? If so, why? How do you think this affects your appearance? Are you familiar with the term Palindrome?

Parents:

- Parents, how can you encourage your children to proactively engage authority?
- What conversations do you have with your child regarding your expectations for them when and if they have an encounter with law enforcement?

Law Enforcement:

- How do you feel when someone is smart mouthing you?
- How do you diffuse a potentially disrespectful situation?
- Why do officers racially profile?

High school intern with Congressman
Bill McCollum. Washington DC

Student Leader:
National Honor Society,
Winter Park High School

Marching band.

GRADE 10

STUDENT NAME	STUDENT NO.	GRADE	DATE
BRYANT, DWAYNE A.	1131771221	10	01/22/86

SCHOOL WINTER PARK SR HI SC SCHOOL YEAR 85-86 SEM 1
2100 SUMMERFIELD, WINTER PARK FL 32789

COURSE NO.	COURSE TITLE	DAYS	GRADE	CREDIT	POINTS
1007330	DEBATE I	103	A		
1001340	ENG II	103	B		
1200310	ALGEBRA I	103	A		
2000310	BIOLOGY I	103	A		
0708340	SPANISH I	103	A		
1302300	BAND I	103	A		
2109310	WORLD HISTORY	103	A		

MEMBERSHIP 90 DAYS | ABSENT 0 DAYS | PRESENT 90 DAYS

↑ ATTENDANCE INFORMATION ↑

STUDENT NAME	STUDENT NO.	GRADE	DATE
BRYANT, DWAYNE A.	1131771221	10	06/11/86

SCHOOL WINTER PARK SR HI SC SCHOOL YEAR 85-86 SEM 2
2100 SUMMERFIELD, WINTER PARK FL 32789

COURSE NO.	COURSE TITLE	DAYS	GRADE	CREDIT	POINTS
1007330	DEBATE I	103	A	1.00	
1001340	ENG II	103	B	1.00	
1200310	ALGEBRA I	103	A	1.00	
2000310	BIOLOGY I	103	A	1.00	
0708340	SPANISH I	103	A	1.00	
1302300	BAND I	103	A	1.00	
2109310	WORLD HISTORY	103	A	1.00	

MEMBERSHIP 90 DAYS | ABSENT 0 DAYS | PRESENT 90 DAYS

↑ ATTENDANCE INFORMATION ↑

GRADE 11

STUDENT NAME	STUDENT NO.	GRADE	DATE
BRYANT, DWAYNE A.	1131771221	11	01/22/87

SCHOOL WINTER PARK SR HI SC SCHOOL YEAR 86-87 SEM 1
2100 SUMMERFIELD, WINTER PARK FL 32789

COURSE NO.	COURSE TITLE	DAYS	GRADE	CREDIT	POINTS
1302500	JAZZ ENS I	103	A		
1302320	BAND III	103	A		
1200330	ALGEBRA II	103	A		
1001370	ENG III	103	B		
2100320	ADV AMER HISTORY	103	B		
0708350	SPANISH II	103	A		
2003350	CHEMISTRY I HON	103	B		

MEMBERSHIP 90 DAYS | ABSENT 0 DAYS | PRESENT 90 DAYS

↑ ATTENDANCE INFORMATION ↑

STUDENT NAME	STUDENT NO.	GRADE	DATE
BRYANT, DWAYNE A.	1131771221	11	06/09/87

SCHOOL WINTER PARK SR HI SC SCHOOL YEAR 86-87 SEM 2
2100 SUMMERFIELD, WINTER PARK FL 32789

COURSE NO.	COURSE TITLE	DAYS	GRADE	CREDIT	POINTS
1302500	JAZZ ENS I	103	A	1.00	
1302320	BAND III	103	B	1.00	
1200330	ALGEBRA II	103	A	1.00	
1001370	ENG III	103	B	1.00	
2100320	ADV AMER HISTORY	103	B	1.00	
0708350	SPANISH II	103	A	1.00	
2003350	CHEMISTRY I HON	103	B	1.00	

MEMBERSHIP DAYS | ABSENT DAYS | PRESENT 90 DAYS

GRADE 12

```
C4453D  01  SPANISH III
C0020D  01  COLLEGE ALGEBRA VCC
00010D  C2  BASIC ECONOMICS VCC
06268D  C3  PHYSICS I
04658D  05  ENG IV
06541D  05  PSYCHOLOGY I
04841D  05  TV PRODUCTION
```

SS85   S1   Band   B   .50
SS86   S1,2 Geometry   B   1.0

```
SY: 86  SCHL: 1411 WINTER PARK SR
CLSS: 540000 01 PERSONAL FIT
SEM1: Y SEM2:    FNL GD: B CRD:  .5

1131771221    GRADE LEVEL: 12
BRYANT, DWAYNE
```

WITHDRAWAL GRADES	DAYS MEMBERSHIP____	DATE			
COURSE TITLE	QUINMESTER ____	GRD	CON	PR	AD
National Honor Society 1986-87					
Social Studies Honor Society 1987					
Spanish Honor Society 1987					
McKnight Achievers 1986-88					

↖ Winter Park High Report Card.
Major transformation after gaining
Knowledge of Self.

Chapter 4
My 4th Encounter: Clash of the Titans

While in college, I was the Student Government Vice President of the North Miami Campus at Florida International University (FIU). I engaged with the campus police many times. Each encounter was always in the capacity of my official duties within student government. All of my interactions were positive and professional. (I want to give a quick shout out and thank the campus police at Florida International University. Your professionalism and concern for student safety was evident and greatly appreciated. Keep up the great work!).

Though I always had positive experiences with law enforcement on campus, I remember one clash with the Miami Police Department that left me with a physical head scar I still have today. In the early 90's, the Haitian community was being vilified concerning the AIDS epidemic. The FDA ruled that Haitians could not give blood due to their high risk of spreading AIDS. They were identified as one of the risk groups that became known as the 4-H club: Hemophiliacs, Homosexuals, Heroin addicts and Haitians. This new policy infuriated Haitians, especially in Miami and New York. They planned protests and demonstrations. This was a major issue during that time, and Haitians were determined to have their voices heard.

Dwayne and Karen: Freshman sweethearts

During this same time at FIU, I fell in love with one of the most beautiful, powerful and intelligent young ladies on campus, Karen Andre. Karen just happened to be the daughter of Haitian music's premier singer/songwriter Farah Juste. The Haitian community in Miami was a proud community. They were vocal and passionate about their beliefs. Since Karen was my "boo", I knew I had to join forces and learn as much as possible about the ruling and get on the front lines with her and her mother. I couldn't let her mother think I was a wuss and afraid to put my life on the line for a cause affecting their community.

The demonstration occurred on a hot day in Miami. The protesters organized themselves as Karen rallied the troops. For some reason, the only Creole words I still remember are: Sak Pase! Nap Bule. The protesters lined up with signs in their hand. The crowd's voice became louder and louder. I remember collective chants of: "Racist... Raaaacist! RAAAACIST!!" I joined in. I even spoke those English words in a Haitian accent. I was caught up in the fever. Karen looked over at me and smiled. That's when I knew I was ready for the front lines. I dropped the sign in my hand and moved to the front of the line. With one nod and a wink, Karen had ignited my warrior gene.

When I walked to the front line, I noticed the Miami Police Department. They stood shoulder-to-shoulder in their dark uniforms – batons in one hand, shields in the other. It was a menacing force, and I was afraid. The people beside me linked their arms with mine and I was locked in. I knew this thing was about to get real. Is this where I really wanted to be? I was on an academic scholarship and wondered if this protest would impact my standings with FIU. What would my momma think seeing me out here? All of those thoughts flashed in my head, and then I began to chant: RACIST!

In that exact moment, I made a decision to protest with my Haitian brothers and sisters. An injustice within the Haitian community was an injustice within the Black American community. As I stood with their community, I felt like I stood up for the rights of all Black people.

For some reason, the people from the back began pushing toward the front. What initially appeared to be a 20-foot distance between the police and protestors, now only seemed like a few inches. Everything became more intense. The police started beating their shields with their batons. Boom. Boom. BOOM! Everything moved in slow motion. I remember one White officer looked directly at me and said: "Go home! This is not where you want to be."

It was too late. I couldn't go home now. I heard him repeat, "This is a final warning! Get back!" Everything in me wanted to go home, but I literally could not turn back.

The sweltering heat, the passion, the chants, the batons, the movement of the police and the movements of the protesters felt like an opposing force waiting to explode. All the sounds were intensifying. My mouth became dry. All of a sudden, a THUMP came from nowhere: Everything went from slow motion to a complete stop. My head started ringing in pain. I reached up to touch the painful area. I pulled my hand back and found it covered in blood. I felt a little dizzy. I looked at the police. They were still in front of me beating their shields. I turned to my left and right and saw my comrades still chanting.

What in the hell just happened to my head? I looked down and noticed two halves of a rock. I picked up one half and held my head with the other hand.

Someone from behind me attempted to throw a rock into the face of the police and it fell about two feet short onto my head. At that very moment, I knew my protest days were over. I tried to be down for the cause, and one of my very own undisciplined comrades hit me in the head with a rock about the size of a grapefruit. I was pissed. I walked off and sat under a tree and watched from afar. The experience felt surreal as I watched everything unfold around me.

I saw agitators from the back trying to hurl things across the line. Why were they so undisciplined? Why would they try to provoke mass chaos? Were they with the protestors or were they purposely trying to wreck the purpose of the demonstration? If one of those rocks had struck the officer's helmet or penetrated his/her face shield, it would have been senseless violence. Excessive force would have been guaranteed.

When Karen came over to me, I looked at her and said, "I tried. I stood with you but my head hurts. I don't want to protest anymore." I gathered my belongings and went back to campus, as the police suggested. I now had blood in the game. It was official; I was willing to stand on the front lines for what I believed in. I do believe on that day God used my head to stop what could have been a potentially dangerous scene for thousands. Sak Pase!

When I reflect back on my college days, one thing I loved about FIU, unlike my small town of Eatonville, Florida, is the opportunity I had to meet people from all over the world! Latin America, the Caribbean, South America, Africa, China and Europe were all represented at FIU. I never knew people were so beautiful and diverse.

Reflections

I believe it is important to stand up for your rights, and if an injustice is committed, then fight for those rights.

Dr. Martin Luther King, Jr. stated, "Injustice anywhere is a threat to justice everywhere." As I look at many of the protests throughout our country, even those dating back to Selma, the protestors consist of many racial groups and ethnic backgrounds.

It seems as though many Americans did not believe the injustices that police officers committed against the Black community in the south in the 60's or even today. Once people began witnessing the brutalities, they realized those injustices were actually happening. Although many people watching the news were not directly affected by police brutality, they knew unnecessary and excessive force within the police force was a threat to all Americans. America is supposed to be greater than that. Today, with the advent of social media and cell phones, people all around the world can see many injustices committed by police and community within seconds of the event.

People are seeing human beings murdered, shot in their backs multiple times or being choked to death by law enforcement. People are beginning to understand that the criminal justice system, from the State's Attorney level down to the police officers on the street, needs to be evaluated and improved. People are also witnessing the blatant level of disrespect toward law enforcement and becoming concerned. Intelligent people desire peaceful resolution and cooperation amongst police and community.

I do believe things will have to get better. Now that the nation is aware of both police brutality and blatant disrespect and killings of law enforcement, we all must work toward a solution. The mentality that police always operate with integrity has been proven wrong over and over again.

The notion that police are only killing innocent, law abiding citizens has also been proven wrong over and over again. If you have an encounter with a police officer and you are committing a crime with or without a weapon, chances are, things won't end well for you.

It is important to comply with the officer, even at the point of arrest. You can advocate for your rights with an attorney and any other legal means necessary after the encounter.

I believe there is a difference between constructively participating in an organized protest and actively committing criminal acts. Protests are a necessary part of the American fabric. From the 1700's to 2015, America has always engaged in organized protests. I have learned that when you are organized and unified with a clear focused agenda for a just cause and you are able to communicate that agenda effectively as you stand with disciplined members amongst your ranks, your voice will be heard.

You can transform your mission into policy. That's how you impact real change. Tearing up your own community by burning, looting and senseless killings will only hurt your own people. Let me ask you this, how can I throw gas and light a match in my living room, steal all the canned goods out of my kitchen and not expect my bedroom to be impacted? It makes absolutely no sense, so let's STOP that madness.

No one gives up power unless the pressure put on them will cost them more than they can afford to pay. Our country has a history of effective civil protest. Engage properly.

For instance, some of the students at the University of Missouri involved in the protest have been my students since fourth grade. They were in the thick of the protest. They found their President of the University to be disrespectful, and many said he did not address issues of racism on campus. They didn't go to his office cursing him out. They organized. Collectively, they joined forces with the football team and other students and faculty. The President resigned. Many of my FB friends did not like that I shared a post about it, but it is an example of organizing your actions and going after a specific goal. It's time to stop burning, looting and destroying other people's property. Tearing up your own community usually doesn't work out so well. Get it?

Parents and Students:

- Should I have participated in the Haitian demonstration?

- Why would one ethnic group or race put their life on the line for another?

- "Injustice anywhere is a threat to justice everywhere…" What do you think about Dr. King's quote?

- When is protesting a good thing?

- When is protesting a bad thing?

- What is the proper way to advocate for your rights?

- What impact does burning down and looting your own community have upon that community?

- If you are stopped by a police officer during a protest, how should you engage with him or her?

Law Enforcement:

- What are some of your thoughts during a protest?

- What happens when protesters start to become violent?

- Is it difficult to keep the peace during a protest?

- What advice would you give to protestors?

Chapter 5

My 5th Encounter: Peaceful Walk turned Bad

When I relocated to Chicago, I lived in the South Loop: Dearborn Town Homes. I loved that community. It is still a great place to live today. During the Taste of Chicago, one of Chicago's major tourist events, I decided to walk past the Buckingham Fountain and over to the Lakefront. I wanted to sit and watch the Yachts cruise on the lake and enjoy the warm night and the nice summer breeze.

I realized it was getting late, so I decided to walk back home. After crossing the street, I noticed many police officers surrounding the location of the Buckingham Fountain. I didn't understand what was going on, so I just walked back the same way I came.

An officer charged over to me and asked, "Where the F are you going?!"

His demeanor and tone shocked me. I had never been confronted so aggressively. The experience alarmed me. I yelled back, "I'm going home!"

"Where do you live?"

"A few blocks away."

"I'm going to ask you one more time," he yelled. "Where in the F do you live?"

I raised my voice in return. "I already told you where I live. I-i-i-i- L-i-i-v-v-e-e- a F-e-e-e-e-w-w-w- B-l-o-o-o-o-o-cks Away!" I replied, drawing out each word in a sarcastic tone.

Uh oh! Things got heated really quickly. Another officer came over, stood directly in my face and cursed at me some more. By this time, I felt afraid for real. It was dark. I was alone with two officers who had plenty back up. In that very moment, all of my senses came back to me. I had to quickly rein in my ego. At that point, getting home safely was more important than defending my ego and being "right."

Although I still believe they were wrong, who knows what else was going on. I asked the officer, "Can I take my ID out and show you where I live?"

His response: "If you don't live where you say you live it's going to be bad for you."

"Yes sir. I'm going to reach into my pocket and slowly pull out my wallet."

I know it sounds crazy, but you better learn how to narrate your movements when dealing with an angry and unprofessional officer. Tell them everything you are doing BEFORE you do it. Ask them if it is ok and wait for their response before making any sudden movements.

Dwayne's Note: Some of my readers asked me if I am teaching my students to be submissive and "bow down" or accept police brutality. My answer is: ABSOLUTELY NOT! Instead, I am teaching them to use wisdom under the current circumstances. It is unfortunate that not all police officers honor their oath to "protect and serve" the communities they work. Even more unfortunate, there is a small percent of police officers who terrorize the communities in which they were sworn to protect and serve. Due to those circumstances, it is imperative we teach our children how to operate in wisdom and strategically engage in the police encounter. There is nothing submissive in teaching students or adults to conduct themselves in wisdom and operate strategically.

There will be a time when police officers will honor their oath to protect and serve. Some call it reform, others call it revolution. Whatever word you choose, time is coming soon where police officers will be professionals who wear their uniform with pride, they will be trained in diversity, mental illness, verbal judo, diffusion techniques and will have an understanding of the communities in which they serve. There will be accountability for their actions within the community.

Since we're talking reform and revolution, let's also add the community into the equation as well. There will also be a time when community members will no longer turn a blind eye to criminals operating with anonymity within the community; there will be a time where drug dealers, human traffickers and child predators will no longer operate without worry of police and community cooperation.

Police need community, just as community needs police.

After pulling out my wallet and showing my ID, the officer said, "well, why didn't you say that in the first place?!" I wanted to say some "nice" words to him and tell that Jack Rabbit "That's what I told your a** in the first place!" Instead I just said, "I thought I told you. My apologies, officer. Can I leave now?" And he abruptly said, "Good Bye!"

After recent police shootings, The U.S. Department of Justice issued a report sighting "reckless use of deadly force" by some police departments. The report uncovered several accounts of police-involved shootings that went outside the bounds of accepted police practice. The justice department stated:

"We... discovered that officers do not effectively deescalate situations, either because they do not know how, or because they do not have an adequate understanding of the importance of deescalating encounters before resorting to force whenever possible."

Some experts say the dialogue that happens between an officer and the suspect is the most important aspect of police work.

Among the U.S. Department of Justice findings[7] were:
- The (omitted) Police department engages in a pattern of using excessive force in violation of citizens' Constitutional Rights.

- Officers were quick to pull their guns, often escalating situations, and fired their guns at people who did not pose an immediate threat of death or serious bodily injury.

- There were incidents where officers punched and tasered suspects already subdued or in handcuffs – sometimes as punishment. And they used tasers too readily.

- The report also cited the city for failing to adequately investigate and discipline the officers involved in using excessive force. They said that investigators conducting reviews admitted that their goal was to paint the accused officers in the most positive light.

7 Danylko, R. (2014, December 8). Examining police training: How officers are taught to deal with armed suspects. Retrieved from http://www.cleveland.com/metro/index.ssf/2014/12/how_police_are_trained_to_deal.html

Perhaps the above actions are those of the shady 10% or perhaps this happened because some police departments do not provide adequate training for their newly hired professionals. When I spoke to Officer Weller of Indiana State Police, he informed me that State Police are amongst the most professional police officers because the total number of training hours in the ISP Academy exceeds 900 (over five months) and after the academy training there's an additional three months of field training before a trooper goes on solo patrol. He also stated training helps officers diffuse situations when someone being detained is communicating in a condescending and belligerent manner. The Indiana State Police are trained to deescalate potentially hostile situations.

If additional training will reduce the amount of senseless shootings, then let's demand police departments spend their additional funds on training and building community relationships rather than purchasing tanks and military grade weapons.

According to Peterson's College Quest - College Education Guidance, some of the minimum qualifications to become a local police officer are[8]:

- Police officer educational requirements range from a high school diploma to a college degree. The minimum requirement is usually a high school diploma, although an increasing number of police departments require applicants to complete at least one or two years of college coursework or obtain an associate's degree. A bachelor's degree is the minimum requirement for federal police jobs. In urban police departments and federal agencies, the ability to speak a foreign language is considered a plus.

- Police Academy Training

- Prior to taking on assignments, police officers go through training at a police academy. The training program generally lasts around 12 to 14 weeks and includes classroom instruction in state laws, local ordinances, constitutional law, civil rights and accident investigation. Police officers also learn about traffic control, self-defense, first-aid, firearms and emergency response.

How to become a police officer - career information, education & degree requirements - Peterson's CollegeQuest.com. (2014, January 15).

When I think about a person with only a high school diploma or even two years of college given the right to detain, arrest or potentially determine the course of my life, I feel VERY uncomfortable. Additionally, 12 to 14 weeks of training doesn't seem sufficient for such an important job.

When I worked in sales for Johnson & Johnson, the company provided a 90-day probationary period, coupled with constant training throughout the year. If there were complaints against our performances that weren't corrected within a certain time period, we were fired. Period! I think there needs to be more educational requirements and training on a national level to become a police officer.

If the educational requirements to become a police officer increased, I believe many of the incidents we see on the news would dramatically decrease. Additional cultural awareness sensitivity training, as well as mental illness training, would produce a well-trained police force and improve police/community engagements and cooperation between the two entities.

Reflections

Parents & Young People:

Whenever authority is present, respect is due even if it isn't shown or reciprocated. When I say respect, I'm not only talking about law enforcement. I am also talking about teachers as well. I was raised to respect adults in general; however, I know in 2015, many adults are not respectful toward young people.

Please teach your child to always be respectful, especially in the case of authority. Authority figures are in a position where they can hurt your child, including teachers. For instance, if your child is disrespectful to the teacher, he/she may have your child sit in the back of the classroom and ignore them, or they may not give them the same grace they give to other students. Believe it or not, all of those actions end up hurting your child because they are not getting the level of instruction and social interaction they should receive from a responsible adult.

Telling them to be disrespectful will also teach them that adults don't have to be respected, even if an adult is trying to help them in life. Eventually, that same disrespect will come home to roost. They will remind you that you told them "not to respect those who don't show you respect." So, when you tell them something as they get older that they think is disrespectful, they will also disrespect you. See how it works?

Respect doesn't mean accepting negative and unprofessional behavior. It simply means being respectful during the encounter and planning an appropriate action that will address the unprofessional behavior in a direct and professional way.

Law Enforcement:

I understand that you all have information that the general public does not. I also understand that you may be responding to dangers that the general public is unaware of; however, what I do not understand is the excessive use of force when the situation does not call for such. Could the officer's have addressed me differently? Was the level of aggression necessary? Was I being profiled? If there was a public danger, was there a better approach?

When officers cross the line of professionalism, it makes the general public want to lash out at you as they lose respect for the badge. It may very well be a double-standard. I guess we hold you to a higher standard than we hold ourselves. I think calmer heads must prevail on both parts.

Though I could be wrong, I also think I was profiled in this situation. Please know that there is a broad range of people in every community. We all have the good, the bad and the ugly. I do believe profiling sometimes makes things easier; however, it never feels good when you are the one being profiled in a negative light, especially if you are not a criminal. Can you imagine what it feels like when you know you are innocent, yet are being treated like a criminal? People staring at you, associating you with criminal behavior. It's a feeling that never goes away.

This book's purpose is to serve as a mechanism for parents and children, teachers and students and police and community. I am promoting real conversations between police and community, then transforming those conversations into positive and proactive behavior that will ensure greater harmony. The STOP is about creating a greater level of respect and peace within the community and police. You are a vital part of our community.

Discussion Questions

- Is it difficult to respect an adult who isn't being respectful to you?
- Who are your role models, and why?
- How can you offer respect even if it isn't given?
- What do you think the community's role is in law enforcement?
- How do you think we can improve Police / Community relations?
- Do you think the criteria to become a police officer is sufficient?
- What do you think is the appropriate professional response to police who use excessive and unreasonable force on the job?

Chapter 6
My 6th Encounter: I May Die Today

After living in Dearborn Townhomes for a couple of years, I resigned from Johnson & Johnson. At the age of 27, I prayed and asked God to help me discover my purpose in life. He revealed my purpose and equipped me to motivate Chicagoland youth and make a difference in the education system.

After giving up a six-figure career, I founded Inner Vision International, Inc. I had no road map for my company. I just wanted to be a force for good within my community. I knew I could motivate young people to discover their maximum potential after helping my first mentee transform from a 1.5 freshman GPA into being a college graduate. I felt that if I accomplished it one time, I could repeat those results on a much larger scale.

In an effort to save money, I downsized and moved to 1212 South Michigan Avenue Apartments. One day I had a lot of to-do items on my list. In a hurry, I rushed down to my car and realized I left my wallet upstairs. Feeling a little frustrated, I returned to the drop-off lane and rushed upstairs to retrieve my wallet. When I returned to my car, I realized I needed to head toward the opposite direction, so I made a quick U-turn to head North on Michigan Avenue. At that time, I drove a Lexus. As soon as I hit that U-turn, I saw flashing lights. I knew the officer was coming for me, so I turned East on Roosevelt and made another right onto Prairie. I purposely pulled into that area because of its new townhomes and high rises, and there was a possibility that someone would record The STOP… just in case.

Two officers jumped out of their vehicle. One approached on the passenger side with his hand on his firearm, the other at my window. Their quick movements caused great concern. Am I really going to get killed over a U-turn? Will I become a statistic or make it home tonight? Why are these two officers harassing me? I thought. This STOP pissed me off.

Truthfully, I did break the law by doing a U-turn, but I felt anxious to see how the encounter unfolded. Right before the officers reached my car, I quickly grabbed my cellphone and called my friend, Hank. I told him, "Dude! I just got stopped. I want you to stay on the phone!"

"Whose car are you driving?" the officer at my window asked.

"Who's driving it?" I replied.

"Do you want to be a smart A**?

"Officer, I am smart actually."

Dwayne's Note: There is a lot going wrong here. As much as I want to say the cops were racist (and they could have been), I MADE THE ILLEGAL U-TURN, thereby inviting them to stop me. I wasn't thinking about that at the time. Neglecting to take full responsibility for my actions, I thought, why are they wasting my time by stopping me? I was already angry and frustrated because I was running behind schedule. The fact that I left my wallet upstairs did not help. Was it possible someone had committed a crime in a similar looking vehicle? Did they stake out my building and thought I was someone else?

Being stopped only made matters worse. I wish I had been respectful before things got out of hand, but in my frustration, I did everything I told you to avoid doing during an encounter with the police. I became disrespectful in my response to the very first question. I intentionally chose sarcasm.

Here's what I forgot to remember: When encountering authority, remain respectful at all times, regardless if that respect isn't returned. The EGO is a powerful thing. When egos begin to rule the conversation and interaction, nothing good usually comes from it. Men: We have powerful egos. If we decided to calm down and think, we could avert much of the violence we see in our communities.

Let's see what happens next during The STOP.

"Is your phone on?" the officer asked.

"Yes it is," I said.

"Hang the phone up!"

"Why do I have to hang my phone up? I will place it on the dashboard."

"Hang up the G.D. phone!" he yelled.

I challenged him. "I don't have to hang up my phone."

"Do you want to escalate this? I can take you to jail right now."

"Take me to jail for doing a U-turn? Really?" I said mockingly.

"Turn off the damn phone right now!"

I wanted to tell him I knew my rights, but I really did not know them. Even if I knew the Constitution well enough to quote it, I knew citing it was not helpful at that moment. They possessed the guns; therefore, they controlled the situation.

I really wanted to keep my phone on. His partner still had his hand on his firearm. The officer's tone and aggressive behavior caused me to fear for my life, but I obeyed and turned my phone off. I probably should have kept my hands on the wheel because of the officer's agitation. I didn't need him to assume I was "reaching for a weapon" while turning off my phone.

"Give me your license and insurance," he demanded.

You know exactly what I did next. I began to narrate my actions.

"Officer, my license is in my wallet. My wallet is in my back pocket. My registration is in my glove compartment. What would you like me to do?" I put my hands on the wheel until he gave instructions. Meanwhile, his partner took his firearm out of its holster.

Let's pause for a minute to discuss the scenario. I felt angry. Helpless. Vulnerable. Scared. Frustrated. And I wanted to scream. I wasn't a criminal, yet they treated me like I had committed a crime. I saw these two White young officers, not much older than me, with their firearms drawn. I burned with anger. I wanted to snap my fingers and wake up from this nightmare.

These are some of the thoughts that crossed my mind:

- I'm in my OWN neighborhood! Was a U-Turn that big of a deal?

- Do these guys just want to kill me?

- Is driving while Black my crime? I don't engage in criminal activity, nor have I, ever. What's really going on?

- Who will explain this to my momma? I don't want to see her cry. What will my brother and sisters think? I have nieces and nephews.

- What will the officers write in their police report? Will they lie? How many times will they shoot me?

- Will the State's Attorney cover up and justify the shooting? Will the police department destroy any evidence? Will the Mayor's office keep this silent?

- I've never been shot. How will it feel? Will I die instantly or will I suffer in pain? Will I see my own blood flowing from my body?

- My God, where are you right now? Can you see me? Can you see what is happening? Is this the destiny that you have for me?

Finally, I told myself, WAIT! I'm not going to die today! I'm not going to die this way. I will not jump out of my car and run. I will not reach for anything and give them an excuse to shoot me. I will not threaten them nor assault them with my words. I have too much purpose within me. These officers are not the only ones who can determine the outcome. I have a responsibility in The STOP as well. I can directly impact the outcome. My greatest weapon in this encounter is complete respect and compliance.

I looked to my left (aka my past) and told myself: I have a long history of accomplishments. I am well-respected, even if these rookies don't know it. I understand who they are and their frame of mind. They will not provoke me into doing or saying something I will later regret. I have a good reputation. I am a good man!

Then I looked to my right (aka my future): I have students waiting for me to motivate them. My business needs me. There are countries I still need to visit. I need to write a book to encourage my students. I need to build a house for my mom. One day, I will have a beautiful wife and children. Yep! I won't be dying today!

Did you see what I just did? I STOPPED. I looked to my left (my past and the officer's state of mind). I looked to my right (my future and my own state of mind). Now it is time to proceed with caution.

When the officer came back with my license, I knew he had no cause to continue with his behavior. However, he told me the car and the registration didn't match.

"Officer that is impossible. I am the owner of this vehicle. I purchased it at an auction and all of my paperwork is in order including my license, registration and insurance. I have done everything you asked me to do. Are you going to write me a ticket for the U-turn or are you going to let me drive away? I am no criminal."

He just looked at me in silence. I probably should have stopped talking right there, but I continued. "Can I have your badge number and last name?"

He yelled his last name and his badge number along with a few expletives. I sat and listened. I had my power back. Apparently, he lost his somewhere. When he finished, I asked, "Was that all?" He forgot to write the ticket and told me to get out of there.

As I drove off, I began to shake from anger, disgust and fear. I felt violated. I wanted to hurt someone – mainly the officer. I went home and sat for a long time. Sometimes, when you are so angry, tears will run down your face. It is better to cry than to hold that anger inside. I grabbed my pillow and yelled into it.

My mom taught my brother and I that real men cry. She told us, "there is more room out than it is in so let it out!" Within minutes, I felt drained. I wanted to say, "goodnight" and start the day all over again.

After a day or two, I went down to the police department and filed an official report against the officer. For a few years after that incident, I no longer viewed law enforcement as police officers. I began calling them cops. I heard more about racial profiling, which fueled my dislike of them.

Due to a court order in November 2015, the Chicago Police Department revealed a long list of complaints against their officers to the public. Now I can check to see if my name is included within the list. Although many people like to say YOLO (you only live once), you have to remember, you have more to live for than to die for. Because "You Only Live Once", you might as well make your life count by taking action when you can.

Interesting STOP Story:

One of my editors for this book, Crystal, told me about the time she experienced The STOP with her 14-year-old brother. As the officer approached her vehicle, her brother decided to search for his cell phone to call their mom. His movement alarmed her. She yelled, "STOP MOVING! WHAT ARE YOU DOING?" She suddenly realized her brother did not understand that any movement during a police stop could result in a possible fatality.

If you do not listen to anything I say in this book, PLEASE listen to this: When/if you have an encounter with a police officer, keep your hands visible. Do NOT grab anything, dig in your pocket or reach inside your coat. Don't even scratch your butt! Keep your hands on the wheel and wait for instructions. And by all means, NEVER run from a police officer. Even if you are innocent, you will look guilty and cause a reaction you do not want.

Reflections

Young People:

When someone is treating you unfairly or being blatantly disrespectful, it is so easy to go toe-to-toe with that person. A Facebook friend of mine sent me a quote from a great book called Proverbs. The quote reads, "Answer not a fool according to his folly, lest thou be like unto him."   This simply means, when someone is loud, belligerent, angry and disrespectful, you do not have to stoop to that level. I'm going to be straight up with you. It's not easy being respectful when someone else is not. Your first thought is to face off with them at their same level. You want to win.

I want you to change the paradigm. I want you to win too. However, winning is not being the biggest fool. Winning is keeping your calm when everyone else is losing his or her heads. Winning is turning away from an argument even when someone is trying to provoke you.

Trust me. This isn't easy. Sometimes I'm able to do it; other times I'm not. You are young! You are Powerful! You are Smart! You can do this! Give it a try. The more you practice it, the better you will become and the more you will grow. Eventually, people will get angry because they cannot get under your skin. That is when you win. You also win when you address your concerns legally.

Parents:

Talk to your children about what I am telling them. Let them know whether you agree or disagree with my statements, and explain why. If you agree with my advice above, then it will be difficult for you to ask your children to behave in ways you are not modeling yourself. They may be quick to say, "Well if being respectful to someone who isn't respecting you in return is such good advice, why aren't YOU doing it?" What will your answer be? What you DO speaks so loudly, your children can't hear what you SAY.

Law Enforcement:

Who was right? Who was wrong? Who has the most responsibility in The STOP? Who has the most training? On one hand, the citizen blames the officer for aggression, and on the other hand, the officer blames the citizen for non-compliance. What was it in this case?

I see where I could have handled the situation much better. Can you see where the officer needed to improve his response in the situation? If we are going to heal police/community relations, we all must take responsibility.

Discussion Questions

- In a stop like this one, are the police officers obligated to back each other up, even if they are wrong? Are the officers expected and trained to remain quiet until the situation settles down, even if she/he sees the situation getting out of hand? At what point should the partner deescalate the situation?

- Do you see why it is so important to keep your hands visible?

- Why is it important to respect the officer, even if you think they are wrong in their words and actions?

- What is an ego? What can you do to keep your ego under control?

- What could have happened if I did not have my driver's license on me?

- How do you win at The STOP?

Chapter 7

My 7th Encounter: Respect is a Two-Way Street

I am excited to share this chapter with you. This chapter inspired the entire book.

In all honesty, this encounter should have been a routine traffic stop; however, when individuals yield to their higher consciousness (many people call it the Holy Spirit), great things are bound to happen. It was this magic that has inspired this chapter. I would like to take you on that journey with me.

As a result of posting this stop on Facebook, the post has gone viral with over a million views. The week prior to posting about this stop, I had about 550 friends on Facebook. Three weeks after the post, I had over 12,000 Facebook friendship requests.

I have a treat for you! I received permission from the Indiana State Troopers to share a link with you that will provide a re-enactment of The STOP. In addition, I had a remarkable opportunity to have a quality conversation with Officer Weller, the State Trooper who stopped me. I will also provide a copy of that link for you. It is a conversation that I always wanted to have with law enforcement. I hope that this will become the beginning of many more conversations and healing between law enforcement and our communities.

Visit www.AboutTheStop.com to view the videos.

Are you ready? Let's go!

I had a speaking engagement on August 31, 2015 at 8 a.m. in the Battle Creek (MI) School District to motivate and inspire approximately 400 teachers and administrators before the new school year. I studied several documents of data concerning the district. After assessing the data, I developed a powerful presentation to motivate Battle Creek's teachers to transform the trajectory of their youth.

In an effort to feel relaxed for the event, on August 30th, I rented a Chevy Equinox from Enterprise Rent-A-Car. I packed my bags, loaded the small SUV and headed out around 4:30pm. I decided to save some time, so I took the Indiana Tollway. I later found out the speed limit goes from 70 mph to a 65 mph zone. (That seems like a little tricky business to me. It must be a speed trap.)

After paying my toll, I was on my way. I remember listening to "Oceans" by Hillsong, one of the world's most recognized worship bands. If you've never heard the song, "Oceans", you should YouTube it. I love the song's middle verse: "Spirit lead me where my trust is without borders... let me walk upon the waters wherever you will call me…. Take me deeper than my feet could ever wonder and my faith will be made stronger in the presence of my Savior…"

I think I had that song on repeat at least four times. I felt close to God; I was in a peaceful place. Soon thereafter, I turned on the regular radio. I wasn't feeling that too much, so I turned on my iTunes playlist. I had the sound synched to the car with the bass on high.

I went to my playlist and set it to "Hypnotized" by Notorious B.I.G aka Biggie Smalls (big song difference, right? Don't judge me!). My foot must have been "Hypnotized." As I came around the curve, I heard the words:

> *"Biggie Biggie Biggie can't you see, sometimes your words just hypnotize me, and I just love your flashy ways, guess that's why they're broke and you're so paid…. Biggie Biggie Biggie can't you*

see, sometimes your words just hypnotize me, and I just love your flashy ways…"

Forget "flashy ways." I looked up and suddenly saw flashing lights. Aww, hell! I hit my brakes, but I knew it was too late. I realized that I was driving 80 mph, so my speed was probably even faster prior to braking. I continued driving, easing off the gas as I looked in my rearview mirror. The officer didn't pull out. Yet. I slowed all the way down to about 70 mph.

Sure enough the cop pulled out. I knew good and well he was coming for me. I was in a Chevy Equinox, so trying to outrun him was not an option or a good idea. I quickly crossed three lanes on the highway to pull over to the roadside. Why couldn't Biggie use another word other than "flashy?" I think he got me this ticket. (Ha!)

As I pulled over, I took my wallet out of my pocket and pulled out my driver's license. Before the officer stepped out of his vehicle, I turned Biggie off. I did not need him profiling me based on my music. Do you follow me on that one?

As the officer walked toward the passenger side, I became a little concerned because they usually come to the driver's side. The last time an officer came to the passenger side of my vehicle, things did not go so well.

The officer leaned down to his left with his hand on his firearm. I instantly knew to put both hands on the wheel. I didn't want to give him any reason to feel like he needed to use his training (aka: pull his firearm). I didn't want his gun to "accidentally" go off while thinking I was "reaching for a weapon."

I wasn't fearful, but let's be for real. With everything happening in America as far as police officers shooting and killing Black men (most cases completely avoidable), I did not feel completely safe.

The officer asked the question that we love so much. "Do you know why I stopped you?"

At first I wanted to say, "Yeeeeeeeees, you wanted my autograph right? You knew who I was and wanted to take a selfie with me." But he was a big White guy, so I decided to keep my jokes to myself. "I'm not sure. I wasn't speeding, was I?"

"Yep. I got you doing 85."

"85! Are you sure that was me?"

"Oh yeah, it was you," he replied. "What's your name?"

I just happened to have one of my brochures on the seat, so I showed it to him. "This is me officer. My name is Dwayne Bryant. I am headed to Battle Creek, Michigan. I have some teachers that I'm going to motivate and get them fired up before the start of the school year. I was so excited to get there. I must have been going over the speed limit."

The Officer's name badge read "Weller." (You always want to know the name of the officer stopping you. It is also great if you can remember the badge number). When Officer Weller asked for my driver's license, I already had it ready.

Dwayne's Note: I did not reach for anything. I appeared calm and not fearful. I showed respect. I answered his questions and requests. Let's imagine for a minute that I didn't have my driver's license on me. (I'd probably be getting ticket for not having my driver license with me and may have had my rental car impounded or even worse, gone to jail). I was already being polite and courteous (not for show. That's just who I am). Let's also imagine if I was rude and disrespectful. Things could have gone wrong quickly.

I am not saying that everything will turn out perfectly just because you show respect. Not necessarily. It all depends on you AND the officer. My whole purpose of this book is to remind you that YOU have a part to play in The STOP. Without question, I believe Black Lives Matter. I also believe Police Lives Matter and in fact, I believe All Lives Matter.

These are some of the actions I followed to help ensure a quality stop after the officer pulled me over:
1.   Remain calm (Turn the music off).

2. Think (Prepare to show your license, registration and insurance).

3. Look to my Left and my Right (envision your past and future (Consider the officer's frame of mind).

4. Keep hands visible (On steering wheel, out of your pockets).

5. Don't reach for anything.

6. Answer police officer's questions.

7. Never argue with police.

8. Never run from police.

9. Comply with police.

10. Do not resist arrest.

11. Learn your rights.

12. Develop an action plan if necessary.

13. Show Respect at ALL times.

14. Make it to your destination safely.

I practice these steps whenever I encounter law enforcement. I would never tell you to do anything that I do not practice on my own. I want you to make it home safely, and I am here to help you do just that.

While Officer Weller was at his vehicle, I realized I was at The STOP once again. You know exactly what I am doing at this point, right? I looked to my left (my past) and thought, I am a 45-year-old Black male. I have no criminal record. I have never been arrested for anything. I am respectful. I have a good reputation. I motivate and mentor children and parents throughout the nation and abroad.

Then I looked to the right (my future). I have a paid speaking engagement in Battle Creek. I will be in Orlando the following week. I am the President of Inner Vision International, Inc. I am necessary on the planet. My momma loves me. She wants to see her baby boy for the holidays. As I am thinking all of these things, I am more aware that I have a responsibility to play in The STOP. My fate is not solely in the hands of this officer; it is in my hands as well.

As the officer came back with his ticket, he asked me, "Do you realize you crossed three lanes of highway without signaling?"

Right there, I thought to myself, aw HELL naw! This is a White code! That's the same thing the officer in Texas said to Sandra Bland. This alarmed me. Yes, I did cross three lanes. And I totally forgot to signal. Where was he going with this? Why did he say that? What is he planning next?

Honestly, I had no clue what was next. I told him, "Officer, when I saw you come out of the median, I knew you were coming for me. I wasn't trying to prolong your stop. I wanted to pull over as quickly as possible so you wouldn't have to follow me too long. I apologize for that. I didn't even realize I didn't signal."

"In the State of Indiana, if you are driving over 20 miles per hour over the posted speed limit, it is considered reckless driving. Here, you can go to jail for reckless driving. I could also write you a $500 ticket."

In my head, I was thinking, Lord Jesus, I need Your divine favor and grace on this stop. I cannot go to jail today. I do not want a $500 ticket, but that's better than going to jail. Father, I do not want someone to find me hanging in a cell a few days later from a "suicide."

Then something told me: It's not going down like that today. My senses suddenly heightened. I became aware of everything. Every sound. At that very moment, nothing else existed except this officer and myself.

All of that flashed in my head before the officer uttered his next words. "I ran your history and everything was clear. You seem like a good guy. I didn't write you a ticket for crossing lanes, and I only wrote you a $150 ticket." I thought to myself, "YES LAWD!" I wanted to jump out of my car, run around and hug the officer. (Now THAT might have gotten me shot so I just sat there).

"Based on everything you said, you didn't have to reduce the ticket down to $150. You didn't give me what you could have and I really appreciate that. Can I take a picture with you?"

"No. Taking a picture of me isn't necessary," he said. "I'm just doing my job. This is what I do every day. Why do you want to take a picture with me?"

I told him I had an opportunity to speak with young people throughout the city of Chicago, the suburbs and across the nation. Many young people believe if a Black man gets stopped by a White police officer, it's going to end badly for them. I told him I just had a debate with my nephew about this topic. My own nephew told me that if an officer pulled me over, despite the fact that I am an educated Black man, I would get shot just like any other Black man because in the White officer's eyes, I'm just "another niggah." (I didn't share that part, but that's what my nephew told me).

"I've told my students that I really believe when you have an encounter with authority, whether you like it or not, you always need to be respectful. Period. This encounter has proven everything I've told them. I want to post this so they can see that it actually worked. Having you in the picture would show them the truth of my statement."

"Do you really get that?" Officer Weller asked.

"Yes. I get that. You are a human being too."

He told me to give him my ticket. I wondered why he took my ticket back. Where is this going? Did he realize he almost let a Black man get off easily? Is this when I get shot? I don't know how many spikes in blood pressure I experienced during The STOP.

Out of the blue, he tore up the ticket. Did you just hear me? HE. TORE. THE. TICKET! I had never seen nor heard of anything like that. I felt both excited and alarmed.

He told me to "sit tight" as he went back to his vehicle. Now I'm thinking to myself, "Dude! This is when you need to just speed off. Drive yourself to a public location. Scream out loud, he's trying to kill meeeee! HEEEEELP!!" It's amazing how our minds can think crazy thoughts if we aren't careful. My spirit had to override my imagination.

Officer Weller came back to the car and said, "I've decided to give you a warning. You're a good guy. You get it. I'm just out here doing my job. Just like you, I just want to go home every day to my wife and child. Have a nice day, sir."

At that moment, I became emotional. A man tear (just one) appeared. (Kind of like that single tear that rolled down Denzel Washington's face in the movie Glory). I placed my head in my hands for a few seconds. Then, I looked sincerely at the officer and said, "Thank You, Officer."

As he drove away, I just sat there and thought about what could have happened. Then I said, "Thank you, God. This was YOUR Grace and Mercy. I love you so much!" I turned Biggie's music off and turned "Oceans" back on… "Spirit lead me where my trust is without borders" resumed playing. As I just sat there for a few minutes, the Holy Spirit gave me the words to post. I wanted to be honest and pure in my communication. This is what I posted on Facebook:

"I sincerely believe, in MOST instances, it is OUR ATTITUDE, OUR BEHAVIOR, OUR RESPONSE that dictates the officers response.

There is so much more to say, but I gotta get back on the road!

#Smiling! #Thankful #GodIS #Please ShareWithOurYouth!"

When I talk to urban youth, many of them are afraid of the police and do not see them as being there to protect them. Instead, they view police as someone who will cause them harm. I once asked a group of fourth, fifth, and sixth graders what they would do if they saw a police car coming toward them. They all said in unison: "RUN." That is a problem.

Some would suggest those students would run because of a predisposition for criminal behavior. That is an ignorant assessment. When young people are fearful and often times lack respect for police, we have to ask why? Just as the community has a role to help repair the trust between police / community relations, the police department has an even greater role. If the relationship is going to heal, law enforcement needs to make some major efforts toward the healing.

When I say major efforts, I'm not talking about asking a few preachers who really don't have a pulse on the community to stand behind the Chief of Police and the Mayor at a press conference and ask for peace and to help build bridges. That is B.S. The community does not respect that because they know it is for show. If the police department was really serious, then they would first police themselves and show that professionalism is their number one priority. They would demonstrate that criminal behavior will not be tolerated, whether it's within the police department or community.

If police officers engage in criminal behavior or criminal misconduct while performing duties, it should not be tolerated from the highest levels. If this was a serious priority, the State's Attorney's office would not take a year to release an indictment, only because a judge ordered tapes to be released. It is very difficult to ask for respect for an organization when that organization illegally erases evidence or ensures it gets "lost" in collection.

Tonight on the news, a reporter stated 10% of Chicago Police Officers have 10 or more complaints against them. How many of those complaints received further investigation? How many citizens received a phone call from the police department assuring them that their complaint would receive a phone call back from the police department within 30 to 45 days? These are examples of basic customer service.

Police are not above the law. When they break the same law they swear to serve, what are their consequences? This is what the community wants to know. If you want to really build trust, you must begin with an honest and truthful conversation, followed by deliberate actions and intelligent policies.

If the community wants to build trust with the police department, then we need to do a much better job as well. We must begin to train our children to respect authority. We must tell them to cooperate and comply with authority. When there is criminal activity within our neighborhoods, instead of protecting the criminal by not "snitching", we need to give that person up to law enforcement. We can't commit criminal acts and then cry when someone gets shot. We can't protest when a White officer kills one of the community members, then remain silent when we kill our own. That is hypocritical. I believe police officers should be held accountable for their level of authority and training; however, the community must be held accountable as well. I'm not trying to take sides in the blame game. I want to take over the entire conversation, transforming it to proactive strategies for establishing positive police and community relations. I want to build safer communities. We are losing far too many precious lives.

Why do we allow a few criminals to terrorize our neighborhoods? We allow drug dealers, thieves, pimps, child traffickers, murderers and pedophiles to destroy our community, and we do not report them. That is the same craziness we complain about within the police department. This Code of Silence must be broken on all fronts.

As long as the community believes the police will not honestly police themselves, and as long as the police know the community will not report criminal behavior and support their presence, trust between the two groups will never exists. If there is never trust, there will never be progress. We are losing far too many precious lives on both sides and it is costing our tax payers Billions of dollars paying for the unprofessional and reckless actions of police officers and criminals within our neighborhoods.

Both parties must agree to full cooperation. We already have plenty of evidence of how a damaged relationship between the community and the police can affect cities. How many more Ferguson situations do we need before we wake up?

Reflections

Being stopped by a police officer can cause a lot of emotions, even if you believe you are innocent. Some aspects of The STOP will be out of your control. I'm excited about this book because I sincerely want parents to have a conversation with their children about the proper way to engage with authority. Not just police, but all authority including teachers, security guards and law enforcement. I want teachers to read this book with your students. Help them develop their thinking and responses in advance. I want faith-based and community organizations to discuss The STOP in a book club and make it available as a life skills manual for your members.

After my Facebook post regarding my incident with Officer Weller, there were some haters who called me all kinds of crazy names. They told me I was going to get Black children killed by teaching them to be submissive to their "White master." I was told I set the Black race back 20 years. HA! That was about the dumbest thing I've ever heard. Respect is never a bad thing. It's honestly something we don't talk about anymore in the proper context. If being respectful will set the Black community back, then I will continue to be even more respectful. Perhaps, we can reset 20,000 years. Respect and integrity are still two powerful character traits. When missing, society crumbles.

I realize some people can only speak from their limited experience or lack of consciousness. My goal in life has always been to be free and to free others in the process. I understand there is a racial climate within America that still lingers. Racism is alive and well. As much as possible, I choose to be free. I want my mind and body to be free from anything that will try to oppress me, even if it's my own thoughts or painful memories of my people's struggles.

During that STOP, there were times when I was uncertain about what was happening, but I never lost faith because I knew that God would never leave me, nor forsake me. I also knew that my destiny was unstoppable. I had to be reminded of that even in The STOP. I believe the best in me brought out the best in the officer. The God in me awakened the God in him, and the outcome was beautiful.

 After Dorothy Tucker, reporter with CBS 2 news, reported on the story, it took on a life of its own. Within a few weeks, members of the Indiana State Police visited my home. Officer Weller, Captain Bursten, Captain Marte' and Tom Triol came to my home along with their videographer to conduct a meaningful interview. The Indiana State Police decided that this story was a great opportunity to better train officers. They wanted to make sure they are proactively training their officers to be more effective in the field, ensuring mutual respect between police and community.

After our conversations, we did a complete reenactment highlighting various aspects of The STOP. Once the interview ended and the cameras turned off, I asked Officer Weller, "So, tell me. Why did you really tear up that ticket?"

What he shared with me confirmed my belief that when we allow ourselves to be guided by the Spirit and not the Flesh, beautiful things will unfold.

His powerful response confirmed everything I knew. There is a Higher Consciousness operating on this earth. Despite many of the ugly things happening throughout the world, we must be the ones to boldly shine the light into the darkness.

Though Dr. King was assassinated, he once stated, "Darkness cannot drive out darkness; only light can do that. Hate cannot drive out hate; only love can do that."

We must find the courage to love one another. If we can't do that, then we must at least find the courage to respect one another. Although there may be a lot of ugly in this world, there is far more beauty if we dare to look for it. If you don't believe me, you can start by looking in the mirror. If you can find beauty there, I guarantee you, you will find it in abundance everywhere else.

After discussing my desire to speak with you about my encounters with law enforcement, my friend Crystal Marshall gave me a challenge to write this book, The STOP, within 30 days. I wrote this book every day, sometimes staying up until 3:00 a.m. When I thought about The STOP's potential to save lives, and the young people, parents, law enforcement and community who could benefit from reading this book, I knew I had to write it. I would not procrastinate on this one. I not only wanted to complete the book, but I wanted to complete it with excellence.

My sincere desire is that this book will be a catalyst towards improving and transforming Police and Community relations.

Mutual Respect

Personal Responsibility

Accountability

Improved Relations

Discussion Questions

- Do you think I began driving differently when listening to Biggie?

- How does music impact the way you drive?

- Does music have an effect on your behavior? Do you listen to music that enhances your behavior in a negative or positive way?

- What do you think would have happened if I treated the officer with rudeness and disrespect?

- Do you agree or disagree with my advice to be respectful to law enforcement, even if that respect isn't returned?

- What can you do to make our communities greater?

- Do you think police officers can relate to the communities they serve?

- How did this officer make a difference by not giving me a ticket?

- Should the officer have followed the law and put me in jail or wrote me up for a $500 ticket?

- What can police officers do to help heal police/community relations?

- How can the community help heal community/police relations?

- What can you do to help heal police/community relations?

- After reading this encounter, is your opinion of police officers the same?

Chapter 8
Expanding the Conversation
(Negative Consequences of The STOP)

Every day we make decisions that will impact the rest of our lives. As young people, decisions are often made based on emotions, the intensity of the moment or sometimes on the pressure from our peers or our family.

Due to many fatal police encounters and police misconduct, respect for the law isn't taught in every household. Here's what you must realize: regardless of whether or not you know the law, like the law, care for the law or respect the law, everything you do is governed by laws. For instance, the Law of Gravity is what keeps you bound to earth. We have the Laws of Physics. There are Metaphysical Laws, Universal Laws, the Law of Cause and Effect and even the Law of Attraction. There are spiritual laws that are higher than these physical laws.

I don't want to get too deep with this, but teaching a child to disrespect the law is teaching that child against the very thing that governs us all. Teaching a child to disrespect the law could eventually lead to criminality. Respect for the law, self, family and community is necessary for a productive life.

One thing I want you to take away from this book is to remember that the decisions you make every day will either enhance your ability to have a successful future or reduce your chances for success. You must intentionally make good decisions. Success isn't rocket science. It is a progression of good decisions throughout your life. It doesn't mean you have to be perfect and make every decision perfectly.

Making mistakes and failures are also a part of growing up, which plays an important role in building your character. However, we cannot continuously make bad decisions, select the wrong friends, perform the wrong actions and expect to get the best outcome. A successful life just doesn't work that way. One wrong decision can change your life forever.

When I define success, it's not always about making money. There are many rich people who lack character and integrity. I do not consider them to be successful. I believe success must have a character component. Integrity must be a part of the success equation. I'm not opposed to you making (legal) money. I just want you to be healthy, wealthy and wise.

The next few pages will show statistics I want you to consider. Please discuss them with your parents, guardians or youth provider. The statistics are based on youth arrests on a national, state and local level. I will also focus heavily on Cook County, primarily Chicago, Illinois. Remember, statistics are simply facts based on what has already happened. You have multiple opportunities to create new and positive statistics every day. You get to choose your future.

As you view this information, I want you to see the impact and consequences of negative encounters with law enforcement. I never want you to be amongst these statistics. Sometimes, we have to see the ugly side of life in order to pursue the beauty. Trust me when I tell you life is beautiful! Make a commitment today that you will explore and experience the beauty in life.

After you have finished reading The STOP, please visit:
www.AboutTheStop.com and share your STOP stories and transformations with me. Thank you again for your time.

Now Go and Be Great!

Dwayne's Note: There is a difference between facts and truth. Again, facts are statistical events that have already happened. It is data based on evidence of an occurrence. Truth is more powerful than fact. Truth speaks to the future, whereas fact speaks to the past. Truth sheds light on possibility for transformation, whereas fact only talks about what or who you have been. Truth allows you to make decisions to change. Facts keep you locked into the past. Truth will set you free from the past. Facts keep you bound. Truth is your divine right. Fact is a trick of the enemy.

So young people, my beloved future, the Truth is up to you. Regardless of your past, the family you were born into, the labels other people place upon you and the negative words people use against you, if you desire transformation strongly enough, you can transcend the facts of your past to live in your truth.

Something to think about

Going to jail also made kids more likely to offend again. Young offenders who were incarcerated are 67% more likely to be in jail (again) by the age of 25 than similar young offenders who didn't go to prison.

- Evidence has found that going to jail as a kid has a "strong negative effect" on a child's chance to get an education.
- Youth that went to prison were 39% less likely to finish high school than other kids who are from the same neighborhood.
- Even young offenders who weren't imprisoned were better off; they were 15 times more likely to finish high school than their incarcerated peers.

Do you see that negative encounters with law enforcement can dramatically decrease your chances of graduating high school? Being incarcerated as a youth will greatly decrease your chances of attending or graduating college. You have to fight for your future! If you live in a major urban city, you must guard your actions even more. There are many distractions and obstacles designed to ensure you never reach success. Some of those obstacles we call family, others we call friends. You must set goals for yourself and develop a plan to achieve those goals. Wishing has never accomplished anything.

Another potential obstacle can be law enforcement. You can't go to jail without being arrested. You can't get arrested without having an encounter with law enforcement. Do you see the connection and reason for this book? If you have that encounter with law enforcement, I want YOU to create the possibility of a positive encounter, both for you and the officer.

Let's talk about gang (aka: organization) involvement for a moment. Some of my students have been in gangs for various reasons. Some because they live in certain neighborhoods and the expectation is for them to join a gang for their personal "safety". Others join because of family tradition. Their families have a long history of gang involvement. Some students had fathers, uncles and cousins in prison. In those instances, prison seemed more like a "situation" rather than a place of embarrassment. Still others join gangs for financial reasons, often involving themselves in the drug game.

They somehow think that they will sell drugs, make enough money and then retire or "go legit".

My friends, please hear me: Very few people accomplish that goal. You must also consider the Law of Cause and Effect. When you sell drugs, you destroy lives and thereby destroy communities. You are killing the hopes and dreams of other human beings, yet somehow, you think you will prosper. God's law doesn't work that way, which leads me to the final Law of Reaping and Sowing. What you give in life is what you will receive. If you plant death and destruction, you will receive death and destruction. Even if you do manage to go legit, those destructive consequences may trickle down to your children. This life must be lived to enhance our families, communities, nation and world – not destroy them.

If you have joined a gang or are involved in destructive behavior, I want you to really ask yourself why you have made those choices. You are better than that. I want you to see yourself as a high functioning human being and as a child of the Almighty. You have a purpose on this planet. You were born for a divine reason. Please don't allow others to convince you to be less than who God called you to become.

Let's look at the cost of juvenile incarcerated populations. How much more could we improve our society if we spent more resources on motivating, educating and inspiring our youth to become productive citizens than incarcerating them?

Cost of an Uneducated Population

- In 2011, Illinois Taxpayers paid an average of $90,000 per year for each youth incarcerated in state prison.
  - In contrast it costs $11,842 to educate a student in Illinois Public Schools
  - 13,432 for Chicago Public Schools
- Tax Payers paid $219,000 per year for each youth confined to the Cook County Juvenile Temporary Detention Center (Civic Federation, 2013)
- Black youth are detained 46 times the rate of their white peers in the Cook County Juvenile Temporary Detention Center JTDC. (National Council on Crime and Delinquency)

JTDC		Youth Prison Data	
85.14%	Black	63%	Black
11.48%	Hispanic	25%	White
2.62%	White	11%	Latino
.30%	Other		
		93%	Male
89.45%	Male	7%	Female
10.55%	Female		

*43% from Cook County
Releases approximately 2,400 youth back into the community each year.*

2013 data compiled by the Illinois Juvenile Justice Commission.

This is how our young people look in the State of Illinois in regards to juvenile detention. Is there racial profiling? Are Black teens being unfairly prosecuted? Regardless of your answer, I think we all can agree there is a disproportionate number of Black (male) youth being incarcerated. We recently learned in a 60 Minutes report that Chicago is the "False Confessions Capital in the United States."[9] Chicago has twice as many forced confessions than any other city in the United States. Learning how to handle encounters with law enforcement is more crucial now than ever before. Parents, mentors, faith-based organizations, community and law enforcement — WE MUST BEGIN THE DIALOGUE! Failure to engage is greatly costing our society.

9 Chicago: The false confession capital. (2012, December 19). Retrieved December 12, 2015, from http://www.cbsnews.com/news/chicago-the-false-confession-capital/

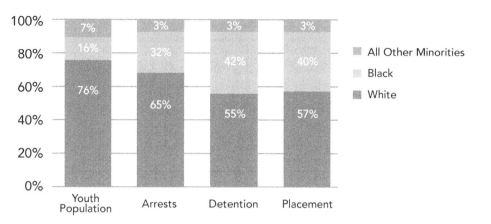

According to the U.S. Department of Justice, Office of Juvenile Justice and Delinquency Prevention:

- "At times, what we want and what is available may not be the same. For our work we used arrest estimates developed by the Bureau of Justice Statistics, which are based on data reported to the FBI's Uniform Crime Reporting Program. These estimates include the annual number of delinquency arrests for persons under the age of 18 for the following racial groups:(1) White; (2) Black or African American; (3) American Indian and Alaskan Native; and (4) Asian/Native Hawaiian/ Other Pacific Islander. With this data it was not possible to study racial disparities in arrest experiences involving Hispanic youth because the available data did not support this distinction (Hispanic identity). So we are limited to the four racial groupings. For the denominator we used population estimates from the Centers for Disease Control and Prevention available in Easy Access to Juvenile Populations.[10]

- Population at risk (ages 10–17): The data was developed by the Centers for Disease Control and Prevention and provides national estimates of the U.S. resident population by demographic subgroups. For the years 1990 and beyond, these data classify individuals into one of five racial groups. This is accomplished by estimating how mixed race individuals would self-identify if they had been asked to pick a single race. These population estimates are available from Easy Access to Juvenile Populations.[11]

- Juvenile arrests: The juvenile arrest estimates were developed by the

Bureau of Justice Statistics (BJS) based on data reported to the Federal Bureau of Investigation's (FBI) Uniform Crime Reporting Program. The unit of count is an arrest, not an individual arrested. This means that a juvenile may be represented in the arrest counts more than once. The FBI reports arrest data in four race groups (i.e., White, Black, American Indian/Alaskan Native, and Asian/Pacific Islander). The FBI does not distinguish Hispanic ethnicity when reporting its arrest data. These juvenile arrest estimates are available from BJS' Arrest Data Analysis Tool.

10 Easy access to juvenile populations. (2004, January 14). Retrieved December 12, 2015, from http://www.ojjdp.gov/ojstatbb/ezapop/

11 Arrest data analysis tool user's guide. (2011). Retrieved December 12, 2015, from http://www.bjs.gov/arrests/resources/documents/adat_user_guide.pdf

Dwayne's Note: This is very interesting. Based on my observations with the previous graph, Hispanic youth are categorized as White. Although many Hispanics identify as White, I think this is very misleading and can lead to inaccurate conclusions. I'm not sure why we can't create a separate "Hispanic" identity. Is this to keep the White population higher? If so, then why the fuss over immigration south of the border? Based upon the chart, Blacks only represent 16% of the youth population, yet 32% of the arrest, or twice the amount of their population in arrests. Blacks also represent forty-two percent of youth in detention, which is equivalent to adult county jail for youth, according to Louisa Nuckolls, Assistant State's Attorney. Placement refers to those who are in residential homes or group homes. It is also important to note that the gender that makes up over 80% of those locked up are males.

Illinois Statewide Statistics

On a national level, 76% of youth are White (due to the large number of Hispanic youth counted among them). We can see the State of Illinois has divided the Youth Population more accurately. Compared to National data, Illinois' minority youth are more disproportionately affected by the Juvenile "Justice" System.

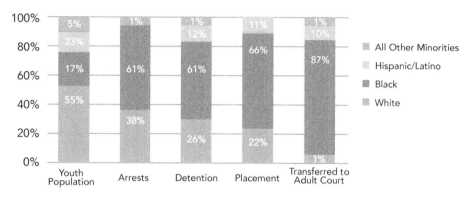

Dwayne's Note: Black youth make up only 17% of the youth in Illinois; however, they make up 61% of the arrests! Are Black youth more criminal in their behavior, or do they get less breaks from law enforcement? Are parents having proper conversations and sharing expectations? Could youth behavior or responses when being detained contribute to the high arrest rates? Were these youth being dehumanized by police officers?

Even worse, in Illinois, 87% of the youth being transferred into adult court are Black youth compared to a mere 1% of White youth. It is extremely difficult for me to believe there is any fairness or any justice in those figures. I don't want to issue a blanket statement; however, it appears to me that the Criminal Justice System is The Criminal.

Parents, mentors, faith-based organizations, community and law enforcement – WE MUST MOVE BEYOND THE DIALOGUE AND BEGIN TO ACTIVELY ENGAGE OUR YOUTH, MALES IN PARTICULAR! WE CAN'T FORSAKE OUR FEMALES.

Cook County Statistics

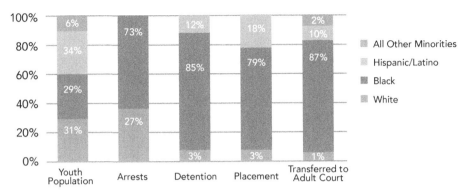

2013 data compiled by the Illinois Juvenile Justice Commission.

Crime doesn't pay... or does it?

JTDC

1.02%	10-12
14.67%	13-14 (7th/8th grade)
24.64%	15 (9th grade)
39.44%	16 (10th grade)
15.30%	17 (11th grade)
4.93%	18 and over

NOTE: Over 78% of youth in JTDC are between 13-17 years old, which represents about 7th grade to 11th grade.

Just when we thought things couldn't get any worse, Chicago proves that's not the case.

While many people are arguing about Spike Lee's movie, ChiRaq, perhaps their voices would be better utilized providing mentoring services and developing better conversations with our young people.

Combined, Chicago's Black and Hispanic youth population is 63%. The White youth population is 31%. Yet, 73% of the arrests are Black. 27% are

White. Does this mean Hispanics do not commit crimes, or are they just not arrested? 85% of all young people in Cook County detention centers are Black.

These numbers are impossible to believe. Blacks, Whites and Hispanics should be angry. It is our taxpayer dollars building more detention centers and less schools or afterschool programs. Actually, Chicago is closing more schools than building them. My organization has developed mentoring programs for various schools for over a decade. I have never sensed that Chicago, nor Chicago Public Schools, were really serious about educating the masses of its youth population. Although Chicago likes to talk about its student achievement, if we investigate further, we will see it is not what it appears.

I am a business man who is passionate about education. As a business man, I must believe the only reason the numbers of incarcerated youth are so high is because there is a profit being made on them. There is some level of industry that benefits from having an uneducated, criminal youth (or overly incarcerated) population. These numbers will not get better without direct, immediate action. The fact that things are getting worse simply tells me that someone or some industry is benefitting greatly.

If the numbers reversed and White kids were incarcerated at such high levels, how fast would policies and laws change? How quickly would the requirement for additional police training become new policy? I remember when Sexting was considered a crime. Many suburban teens were charged with criminal activity. Parents understood the long-term impact and the laws changed.

How could such devastation happen to our young people and NO ONE has sounded the alarm on a tactical level? Do Black Lives Really Matter? Or does it only matter when we are killed by a White police officer?

From experience, the solution isn't rocket science. From 2005 – 2010, my company Inner Vision International, Inc. partnered with Matteson SD 162 and dramatically improved that district's school climate, thereby reducing suspensions, eliminating expulsions, quadrupling parental involvement and improving students test scores, even at a time when the demographics were shifting dramatically. If we are going to change these statistics, it will require real leadership and commitment.

I've been in Chicago since 1995. Based on the stats above, I am convinced, with few exceptions, either Chicago does not have the leadership within itself or it lacks the commitment to positively affect the change necessary to transform its youth population. Until that changes, we will continue to have the same outcomes.

Detainee Charge Information

35.93%	Warrants (Violation of Probation)
9.91%	Unlawful use of a weapon
9.95%	Robbery / Burglary
12.21%	Drugs

NOTE: Over 78% of youth in JTDC are between 13-17 years old, which represents about 7th grade to 11th grade.

More to think about...

NIELSEN is a leading global provider of information and insights into what consumers watch and buy. They also study media consumption: television video games, radio, social media, etc.

- African Americans consume approximately seven hours, 12 minutes of media per day.
- 40 percent more than whites (five hours and two minutes per day).
- Hispanics consume approximately 5 hours and 30 minutes of media per day.

Parents! Increasing our children's academics is NOT rocket science. Let's give our young people a fair chance at real success. You have to ensure they are consuming less media and are reading more, doing homework more and exercising their brain power in a positive and constructive manner.

Young people, in many ways adults have failed to guarantee that you will have a brighter future than their own. I apologize to you for the lack of leadership within many communities; however, failure must not be an option for you. I want you to mobilize yourselves around an academic and social agenda. That means less time and energy on mindless social media and more time developing a plan to enhance your life and society in general.

You have to tell your peers about the importance of education and respect for authority. I have an array of materials that will help you along your journey. My organization has developed and implemented evidence-based curricula and results-oriented mentoring programs for more than 15 years. All of our curricula are designed to motivate youth towards their maximum academic and social achievements.

I hope you have gained insights that you can use immediately. Thank you for taking this journey with me. Together, we can ensure a positive relationship between self, family, community and police.

Appendix

Lastly, I want you to see what happens when parents do not parent. When schools fail our children. When cities, states and the nation neglect educating our youth and decide to incarcerate them instead.

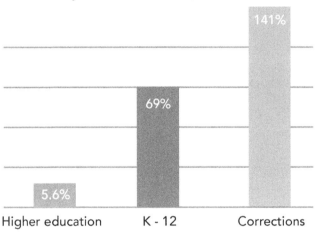

Source: CBPP analysis data from National Association of State Budget Officers.

Center on Budget and Policy Priorities[12] released a report that shows the growth of state spending on prisons in recent years has far outpaced the growth of spending on education. After adjusting for inflation, state general fund spending on prison-related expenses increased over 140 percent between 1986 and 2013. During the same period, state spending on K-12 education increased only 69 percent, while higher education saw an increase of less than six percent.

The report suggests that states' spending practices are ultimately harming their economies, while not making the states safer. The authors conclude that if "states were still spending the same amount on corrections as they did in the mid-1980s, adjusted for inflation, they would have about $28 billion more available each year for education and other productive investments."

12 Mitchell, M., & Leachman, M. (2014). Changing priorities: State criminal justice reforms and investments in education. Retrieved December 12, 2015, from http://www.cbpp.org//sites/default/files/atoms/files/10-28-14sfp.pdf

Prison Facts:

From less than 300,000 inmates in 1972, the jail population grew to 2 million by the year 2000. In 1990 it was 1 million.

One of the fastest growing industries in North America?

The prison industrial complex is one of the fastest-growing industries in the United States and its investors are on Wall Street.

Systems are in place for failure.

There are approximately 2.5 million inmates in state, federal and private prisons throughout the country. According to California Prison Focus, "no other society in human history has imprisoned so many of its own citizens."

The figures show that the United States has locked up more people than any other country: *a half million more than China*, which has a population five times greater than the U.S.

Statistics reveal that the United States holds 25% of the world's prison (slave) population, but only 5% of the world's people.

Bonus Material for my Young People
(The Chapter that Didn't Make the Cut)

After a very competitive interview process during my senior year at FIU, a Cuban woman named Martha Mestril hired me to work as an intern with Johnson & Johnson. Martha reminded me of my own mother. Due to her hard work ethic, professionalism, strict adherence to company policy, passion for life and career guidance, Martha became my Cuban mother.

After graduating FIU, I embarked upon my sales career with Johnson & Johnson. I began working with J&J in Miami. Many of my accounts would not speak English to me. Fortunately, I studied Spanish for a few years in high school and in college. Being able to converse in Spanish proved to be an asset in my career.

Note: If you are taking a foreign language, I highly recommend you take it seriously. Spanish is a great language to learn. If you are able to learn Mandarin (Chinese), please do it! When I travel throughout America, Africa or the Caribbean, people speak languages other than English. It is essential to learn an additional language.

While at Johnson & Johnson, I was promoted from Miami to Detroit, and then promoted to St. Louis. After two years in St. Louis, I was promoted again and relocated to Chicago. In St. Louis, I met a gentleman by the name of Sharone Hopkins. When I first met Sharone, he was a child of the State and lived in Echos children's home. He had a 1.5 GPA, sold drugs, and I believe, he may have had some gang affiliations. His parents were not a positive active force within his life.

Within the two years of serving as his mentor, Sharone transformed from a low performing student to a young man who desired success in life. Establishing the connection between his present condition and the future he desired, we developed a plan to create a successful future. Sharone has since graduated college, studied in Ghana, traveled the world and is a productive citizen in society. When my father came to visit me in Chicago,

Sharone drove all the way from St. Louis to visit with us.

I share this story to tell you that if you decide you want to become success-ful in the right way, success is possible, despite the family you grew up in or your past. If you do not have positive examples or role models within your own family, find someone who believes in you and can help you develop a plan for success. Sharone was a blessing to me as I was to him. I traveled to Egypt because he invited me to tour with his church. It was awesome because I saw all of the wonderful things Mrs. Bey taught me about Egypt at Winter Park High School.

I have discovered many of my students wish for success. Wishing is just hoping for something without putting any effort into its attainment. I tell my students they have to move from a wish to a dream. From a dream to a goal. From a goal to a strategic plan. From strategic plans to accomplishments. Do you see? Simply wishing never accomplished anything!

The other thing you have to STOP banking on is "potential." Many people use this term frequently. I hear parents and students brag about their po-tential. Well, let me share something with you I learned in middle school. There are two kinds of energy: potential and kinetic. Potential energy is like the rock on top of the hill. It is not moving. It is dormant. It lacks motion; therefore, it has potential energy. Now, if you push that rock down the hill, that energy changes from potential to kinetic energy. Kinetic energy is ener-gy in motion. It is moving and accomplishing something.

Can you see it now? When you say you have potential, it simply means you are not doing much of anything. You know good and well you could im-prove yourself right now. So let's not make any more excuses for potential. "F" Potential. That means "Forget Potential." Let's get moving toward our dreams!

Another thing: Don't let living in the hood make you think you are hood! You are Kings and Queens. It is time to BE who you are – not who someone told you to be. Explore your history, and you will find great pride in your-self. BE who you are. You have my permission.

Also, be careful of the music you listen to. I was driving down 47th street and observed a girl with headphones on singing a rap song. The song must have been about killing, and "drankin" and "smokin" because she kept saying, "I'm a killa; I smoke and drank" repeatedly. I thought to myself, she doesn't know the harm she is doing to her mind. She is literally programming her mind to accept that as her truth. That is NOT her truth.

In all likelihood, it probably is not the truth of the rapper either. Many times, rappers make that stuff up in order to sell more units. Don't allow them to get rich by selling you garbage!   Demand more from these artists.

Since I am on the subject of music, I might as well tell you this story. One day, I took my car to the Mercedes shop on Diversey in Chicago. I noticed a lot of guys headed to the top of the building. I asked, "What's going on?" Someone told me they were shooting a music video. I assumed the guys headed to the top of the building were shooting videos with nice Mercedes. They had fine women, gold chains and all. I decided to wait for my car.

At some point, the guys came back downstairs. I chuckled because they got in Chevys and Fords while I drove away in my Mercedes. Nothing is wrong with driving Chevys and Fords. I rent them whenever I travel. So what am I saying? I am saying, a lot of the images you see in music videos and TV aren't real! That's why they call it TV…Television — Telling You a Vision of what they want you to believe. So many young people have no clue that most of these so-called rappers aren't even making six figures. They are still living at home with their momma's because they cannot afford to move out.

Yet, they show you big mansions, yachts, fast cars, bling jewelry and fine women. Guess what? Can I tell you a secret? Put your ear closer to the book. A little closer because I'm going to whisper this to you: All of those material items are rented. That's why it is foolish to pursue material items without pursuing your education and developing strong characters. All of those material items will fade. Who you are as a person will last forever. That's why you want to become the best version of yourself.

Interesting STOP Story:

A good friend of mine, Adrienne, does accounting for the movie industry. I'm talking about big Blockbusters. She has also done the accounting for various music videos. She told me that almost always, EVERYTHING in the video is rented: The women – Rented. The cars – Rented. The houses – Rented. The jewelry – Rented. The Yachts – Rented. The furniture – Rented. The money – Rented. Even the doggone pit bulls are – Rented. HA!

Can you believe that? Many of the images they project are not real. Young people, I do not mean to disappoint you, but I would rather you awaken to reality than be lullabied with an illusion.

Why am I bringing all this up? What does this have to do with The STOP? The music you listen to has an impact on your behavior. It can either limit or stimulate greatness within. It has been proven that what you allow into your mind has a direct impact on your life. In our Power of Words curriculum, we discuss the Law of Cause and Effect, which states the following:

> *Watch your thoughts for they become your words.*
> *Choose your words for they become your actions.*
> *Understand your actions for they become your habits.*
> *Study your habits for they will become your character.*
> *Develop your character for it becomes your destiny.*

Therefore, you must guard your mind and not let anything negative into it. I hope this is food for thought. Please speak more about it with your parents.

Before you close this book, I want you to remember this: Whether you encounter The STOP once or five times, you possess a greatness inside of you that no one can take away. I challenge you to draw from your own strength and make the best decision in every situation. You were born to make a difference.

Special Thank You's

My beautiful mother

Bill Farley, CEO Farley Industries

Indiana State Police, especially Officer Aaron Weller!
Martina Smith – PR / Social Media Expert
Camille Bradshaw – CEO, Producer, Brand Developer
Amber Harvey, Flow Editor
Chrystal Bethell, Model, Actress, Content Editor
Crystal Marshall, CEO of Write to Success, Inc. – Editor
Dayna Sanders – Content Provider, Educator
Kendra Y. Mims-Applewhite – Copy Editor
Tim Fullerton, Graphic Designer
Katara Patton - Final Editor
Renee Collins - Accountant
Juan Pena, Recording Engineer
Louisa J. Nuckolls, Assistant State's Attorney
Captain Dave Bursten, Indiana State Police
Dorothy Tucker, CBS News – Anchor
Jamal Jackson, Attorney
Terence Crayton, Awesome Photographer, Great Mentor, Friend
Derrick Young, CBS 2 – Traffic Reporter, Friend
Priestly Williams, Videographer
My biological father, James
My siblings
Mr. & Mrs. Williams
My greatest educator, Barbara Bey
All Educators who have invested and believed in me
John Warford, Greatest College Mentor
Martha Mestril, my Cuban mother

Ozzie Ritchey, my college mother
Dr. Blondean Davis, Superintendent who believed in my ideas and supported my career for over a decade
Anita Andrews, my Chicago mother
Florida International University – Greatest University known to mankind

Everyone else I forgot

God

Made in the USA
Monee, IL
18 September 2021

78346456R00075